A Missionary Family in Nigeria and Uganda 1936 – 1964

Martin Wyatt

THE DERWENT PRESS
Derbyshire, England

www.derwentpress.com

A Missionary Family in Nigeria and Uganda 1936 – 1964

By
Martin Wyatt

© 2006 Martin Wyatt

ISBN 1-84667-026-8

Cover art and book design by:
Pam Marin-Kingsley
www.far-angel.com

Published in 2006 by

**The Derwent Press
Derbyshire, England**

www.derwentpress.com

Contents

Acknowledgments

I am grateful to SCM-Canterbury Press for permission to quote the extracts from J H Oldham's book, Florence Allshorn and the Story of St Julian's, SCM Press 1951.

I have been much assisted by staff of the Special Collections at the University of Birmingham, where the Church Missionary Society archive is housed. Unfortunately the Church Mission Society has not responded to my requests to use the material in the archive. This account therefore makes no direct reference to anything for which that archive is the sole source of information, and this has some effect in reducing its value.

I am grateful to members of my family for their comments on a previous draft. My special thanks to my cousins Lynne Dixon, who in addition to commenting, provided a copy of a section of her mother's diary, and Janet Hughes, who responded to enquiries. I am also grateful to everyone else who commented on the previous draft.

A Missionary Family in Nigeria and Uganda 1936 – 1964

Introduction

The story of my parents and their family says much about the life of English missionaries in Africa around the middle of the twentieth century. I have constructed from their own writings and some other material an account not of their achievements, but of a particular way of life and its effect both on the families they were born into, and the family they created. The narrative backbone is my mother's autobiographical memoir, written in her eighties, but the real value comes from the contemporary letters written between her and my father. These materials are supplemented by some other papers of theirs, by what I have gleaned from the CMS archives, and by what I remember myself. References to the books mentioned in the bibliography help to put the story into context. In writing her memoir, my mother does not seem to have referred to the letters, and consequently made the occasional error, but they overwhelmingly support the accuracy of her memory. The nature of the material means that there is more about the periods my parents were living apart than about their life together.

This compilation is an attempt to understand the past. Although it is mostly my own past, much of it now seems strange to me. Here was a way of life that I was brought up in, took for granted, and in consequence hardly tried to understand. Now that I do try to understand it, I do so with a mingling of gratitude, resentment, embarrassment, and a great respect for my parents. My father in particular was an interesting person, emerging from a working class background in a highly stratified society to gain the confidence and esteem of many different people in completely different cultures.

Although it is an attempt at understanding, the account that follows is essentially a selection and arrangement of raw material, with very little interpretation, apart from the final section which offers my own reflections. Most of the material falls into two categories: contemporary letters and my own and my mother's memories. My mother's autobiographical memoir is given in full, but the rest has been selected, and much of the selection has been summarised; so it will be as well to say what has been at the back of my mind in making the selection.

Some personal material has been included, because I want any reader to meet two particular people. Some very intimate details have been omitted, and I have put in stories of ordinary human interest. For the most part, however, I have aimed to select what is of interest to anyone wanting to understand the period, particularly anyone wanting to understand the lives of missionaries at that time, their daily patterns, their motivation, their dilemmas, the conditions they came from and went to, and their relationships with each other, with government, and with the people they aimed to serve. I know that I have put in bits which tend to show my family in a good light, but I have not deliberately left out anything which might show it in a bad light.

If my mother had enlarged on her memoir to produce something more like the present compilation, it would almost certainly have been full of the names of the colleagues who meant so much to her. I have read several books like that, and did not find them interesting or valuable, so that is not what I have put together.

One peculiarity of my parents' relationship was that both were invariably known to each other and to their friends and acquaintances by nicknames. My mother, born in 1907, was christened Edith Victoria, but from a very early age was known as "Don". My father, born in 1912, was christened Alfred Ernest but from some time uncertain was known to everyone except his father, sister and brother-in-law as "Rex." They are referred to by these names from now on.

The first part of this narrative follows Don's life from birth to the end of 1938. In January 1939 she sailed for Nigeria. Part two follows Rex's life, in less detail, until the same period. Part three covers Don's early life in Nigeria and her meeting with Rex and eventual engagement. The memoir and letters permit an interesting description of missionary life in a fairly isolated situation. Part four deals with their marriage in South Africa, Don's stay in South Africa, and their eventual return to Nigeria. Part five covers the rest of their time in Nigeria, and in this section there is towards the end a general description of life in Lagos (and, marginally, elsewhere) covering the period 1944 to 1951. Part six covers their time in Uganda. Part seven is an afterword.

Don's narrative is given in a different type face.

Part 1.

Don Parker

1907 – 1938

The story of Don and Rex Wyatt starts in 1907 with the birth of Don, the first child of Frederick Joseph Parker, Commercial Traveller, and Edith Marie Parker, formerly Wise. She gives a lively account of her early years.

My first memories are of the house where I was born—49 Edric Road, New Cross, London SE14, a terrace house of 7 rooms, a scullery, outside loo and garden. I was the eldest of four children, all born within four years ten months. When my younger sister, the youngest child, was born I was taken to stay with friends in Bermondsey and can remember very little of that time except that I was fascinated by the moss which grew in the garden. I remember the night that Connie, the youngest, had convulsions and the doctor was called. *[The other children were Frederick and Nora.]*

I had been named Edith Victoria after my mother and, I suppose, Queen Victoria, who had died six years before my birth. However, I was never called Edith or Edie. The story was that when I began to speak I said "give me" quite often and my mother changed it to the French *"donnez moi."* Then I was called Donnie or Don. Even though I started off school with the name Edith, there was another Edith Parker in the same form and I soon became Don, so all my life I have answered to that name.

When we reached the age of five, we all went to school, Monson Road London Board School, at the end of the road. At the other end there was the South Eastern Fever Hospital. In the first class we were taught by Miss Bird, who was always called by the children "Miss Dicky Bird." One incident whilst in that class remains in my memory. Olive Stringer, who lived next door but one to us, managed to insert a bead into her ear and I was asked to take her home. We played with sand and water on sand trays, and beads for counting, and we learnt our letters and numbers with chalk on slates.

I liked school and managed to do well in exams as I progressed up the school. We were fortunate in having an Art Room ruled over by the Art Mistress and I always enjoyed these lessons. Singing lessons and plays were also favourite subjects. It was thought I had a good singing voice and I sometimes sang solo at school concerts. Classroom exams did not bother me, but when came to the entrance exam for a secondary school I went to pieces and never did well enough to pass. That was after the trauma of the air raids which affected me nervously.

When I was seven the First World War started. My father who was then 33 was "called up", but as he had flat feet was not sent to France but to Colombo, Ceylon. He was away for three years and was a stranger to us when he returned.

I remember the First World War years very vividly. My mother was asked to take over my father's job. He was a representative of the wholesale confectionery firm Southwells of Dock Head, London. This entailed travelling with samples to "high class confectioners" in

London, Surrey and Kent mainly, and collecting orders. It meant leaving us children with anyone my mother could hire to look after us while she was away. Sometimes when we had daytime air raids I was worried about my mother's safety. At one time my mother's mother and sister, Beth, lived with us, and another time my father's mother and married sister. This put a strain on family relationships.

Looking back I realise we were deprived during those war years and were sometimes hungry. There was strict food rationing with ration books of food coupons as well as clothing coupons. As the eldest it was often my job to stand in queues for meat, fat, sugar, etc and we never seemed to get sufficient sleep with air raids night after night. The Germans were trying to find and bomb the Woolwich Arsenal where munitions were made, and in the early days zeppelins and later planes passed over and dropped bombs, disturbing our nights. One night a bomb was dropped in the playground of our school at one end of the road and another in the laundry of the hospital at the other end. We tried various ways of taking shelter. At first under the old grand piano. Then in the cellar of our house. Later with many neighbours in the basement of the fever hospital, where it was very warm due to the hot water pipes heating the wards above. It did not occur to us at the time that if a bomb had been dropped and penetrated to the basement, many of us would have been scalded. My mother must have been living under considerable strain during those years, working during the day having had very little sleep, with all the responsibility of caring for four children. This period also took toll of my own health and I became a very nervous child. My hair came out in patches which was diagnosed as *alopecia aereta* and persisted for some time whilst undergoing treatment at the Blackfriars Skin Clinic. My nervousness was the main reason for my being unable to pass external exams.

When the war was over my father came home. We had to adjust to having a man in the home, and he was "uncle" to us for a time. My mother and father decided to have a second honeymoon, and the four of us children were put on a train to Poole in the care of the guard. My father's sister and mother lived at Poole. Our aunt's husband was a merchant seaman and was at sea whilst we were there. They had no children at that time and my aunt was very strict with us. After a fortnight we returned to London and settled into family life and my father returned to his former job.

I was very happy at school both at lessons and at recreation. We played netball, and I was in the school team, playing home and away matches, and on sports days I entered for the high jump and running.

When I reached the top class in the school I was elected Head Prefect and of course had duties appropriate to that position. In this class I won several prizes for essays on subjects set by the RSPCA.

Although I had been unable to pass the entrance exams to a secondary school, I did get a free place to a Commercial College in central London. For some reason my parents decided to refuse this; it might have been because of the daily journeys to and from the city. Instead I was sent to the South Eastern Commercial College in the Camberwell road, where I learnt shorthand and typewriting. After a few months I got a job in the office of Holdrons of Peckham, a big department store, and continued my lessons at the South East Commercial College at evening classes. When I was considered proficient my father's brother, Alfred, caused a job to be found for me in the office of his paint manufacturing firm, Endurite Ltd, which was within easy walking distance of my home. After about two years the firm got into deep water financially and I, with others, was made redundant. For two weeks I had a temporary job with a building firm in Silvertown, which meant travelling on a tram through Blackwall Tunnel. When I had just about learnt all the building terms, the girl I had replaced returned.

Through the Unemployment Bureau I obtained a job as shorthand typist in the firm of Bevan and Bassett, Tinplate Brokers, in Great Tower Street opposite the great Tubby Clayton's Church, and I worked there for about two years with one other older woman. We had many a laugh together, especially over Mr Bassett, who very often used to come in from lunch not exactly the worse for drink, but rather merry. In the lunch hours I walked in the gardens of the Great Tower of London. During the Great Strike several times I walked from New Cross to Great Tower Street.

When I felt I needed a different job, Vera Patterson, who worked for the Irish Church Missions in Buckingham Street near Charing Cross Station, spoke for me to Mr H H Martin, Secretary of the Lord's Day Observance Society, also in Great Tower Street, and I was taken on as his secretary. I stayed there until January 1936.

We had all been sent to Sunday School at All Saints Hatcham, our parish church, and I graduated into the Girls Bible Class led by Nan Thurnell, with whom I became very friendly. At fifteen, I was prepared for confirmation by the Vicar, an elderly rather pathetic man who, it was rumoured, drank heavily, and confirmed at the neighbouring St Catherine's. The services at All Saints were very uninspiring and soon after Confirmation I started attending St George's Brockley, daughter church of St James, Hatcham. I was soon taking part in St George's church life. At this time I taught in the Sunday School of St Michael's, another daughter church of St James, Hatcham. There I met Julia Leakey, who later married the curate of St James, Laurence Barham. After marriage they went to Ruanda with CMS. When I was about sixteen, Nan Thurnell married Fred Hammett and I became god-mother to their first son Peter John. They moved to Streatham Vale where I often visited them. Through the Scripture Union meetings at St George's I met Grace Cave the leader and she became my closest friend until she died of cancer in 1936. Her fiancé had died and she lived with her father and mother in Brockley. I quite often stayed with her whilst her parents were on holiday and we had several seaside holidays together. She left me her engagement ring and £200.

She and I also went to the Keswick Convention in 1924. The meetings in the huge tent greatly impressed me and at one of the missionary meetings I felt impelled to stand up with those who declared they would go out as missionaries if the way opened up. This resolve was strengthened by a missionary exhibition held at St James Hatcham where there were stalls manned by missionaries from China, Japan, Africa, the Sudan and India, who had exhibits to illustrate the talks they gave on the country of their adoption. I also took part in one of the plays which were given from time to time each evening. This exhibition was very well attended, in fact crowded at times. I attended every evening and the whole exercise made a great impression upon me, so that in spite of years of waiting I never lost the desire to go abroad as a missionary.

Some years after she had written this, I asked my mother why she had decided to become a missionary, and she replied in almost the same words about the Keswick Convention. Clearly this was a key episode in her life, but the period that followed was in some ways quite difficult. She continued living with her family, sharing a bedroom with her two sisters until she was 28.

When I was twenty the family moved to Thornton Heath. I had heard of Christ Church West Croydon as being a lively church and on the first Sunday I attended there. It was within easy walking distance of my home. A member of the congregation, Mrs Butler, noticed that I was a stranger, spoke to me and invited me to tea. There I met her son, Bill, who was later ordained and went out to Ruanda with Nancy, his wife, who was also at the tea party.

I soon settled into the life of Christ Church, joining the Young People's Group and the Badminton Club, and taking a Sunday School class and later a girls' Bible class which was held in the vicarage. St Christopher's, the daughter church of Christ Church, on a new housing estate, had a Guide Company run by Nancy Breary. She asked me to be her lieutenant, a job I did until I went to Weybridge, although I had not previously been a Guide. At the same time, having advised CMS of my desire to go abroad, I was advised to study with the Home Preparation Union as my syllabus, and Joyce Bailey, our curate's wife, who was on the Candidates Committee of CMS was asked to be my tutor. Joyce and Bill lived in a flat on the London Road, West Croydon, and we spent many an evening discussing and talking our heads off. This was a very happy period of my life, not least the Bank holidays when the young people rambled in Kent and Surrey, and the times when

Clifford Martin, our vicar, took a group of us sailing on the Norfolk Broads, which in those days were very peaceful with very few motor launches. We hired two yachts, to divide the sexes at night, but during the day we mixed the crews.

After Clifford Martin had moved to be vicar of Christ Church, Folkestone, Parry Jennings became our vicar. Aubrey Hopkins, always called, "Hop", in charge of St Christopher's, daughter church of Christ Church, moved to a living, and Fortie Ross came as curate in his place. Fortie later went to Maseno, Kenya, with CMS.

In 1934 *[actually March 1935]* I offered to CMS and was given an interview by the Candidates Secretary. After filling in forms about my belief etc, going for interview to three clergymen and going before the Candidates Committee, I was accepted for training. During the interviews it had emerged that I had a fear of illness, that is of seeing ill people, and it was thought advisable for me to have some experience in a hospital. In January 1935 *[this date must be wrong]* I went as a probationer to Weybridge Hospital in Surrey. This was a small hospital with wards of twelve beds each for men women and children, and six single rooms for private patients. I worked there a 14 hour day, with a full day of duty once a fortnight and half a day off in alternate weeks. Probationers had their own room and were paid 10/- a month and full board. It was very tiring work but I was happy there and learnt a great deal. I had never seen a dead person before going there and at first I was greatly distressed, especially when I discovered a baby of nine months who had died in her cot. During the fifteen months I was there I had my own appendix removed, but was soon able to return to duty.

I left Weybridge Hospital in April 1937, had a fortnight on the Broads with Clifford s party, and in May went to Kennaway Hall, Stoke Newington, the CMS Women's Training College. It was all very strange at first but I soon made friends and it opened up a new world to me. I had never met anyone like the Principal, Florence Allshorn, but I was ready for her teaching and lapped it up.

Florence Allshorn was evidently a person who made a strong impression on people from many different backgrounds. She believed in training the whole person and in enjoying life, but she also believed in not being preoccupied with self. In Don's copy of *Florence Allshorn and the story of St Julian's* by J H Oldham some extracts from Florence's writings have been marked, dealing mostly with that ideal of selflessness:

"For most people it is a very slow, long, arduous business, the business of being re-born, the endless day to day struggle to find God, to come nearer to God, to think and will more and more exclusively as He thinks and wills; and to be partners in Christ's redemptive work."

"It is only as we vow ourselves to obedience that we begin to see that we, as we are, can never enter this fresh, free, utterly lovely Kingdom of heavenly love. That takes us a long time because of the 'I' ingrained in every beat of our heart, every movement of our minds, every habit of our habitual day;—slowly, by determined will, we have to empty ourselves. When humility is there, we start really following, but not before. It is the first obedience; to disobey the order to be humble turns us into Pharisees, hypocrites, and pious prigs."

"I hope all goes well with you. It will when the 'I' is taken out. Not till then. When you really see that so deeply that you are acting a little on it, you wonder why on earth you clung to that little puffed-up

13

being so long. The release and clearness of the joy is so different and the peace at the centre of you. I know that I shan't let you rest till you do."

And in a passage about the consequences of failure:

"If a woman fails to adjust her emotional life and goes on unconsciously working with a sense of failure there, then the one spot where she can find success is in 'the job'; but the almost inevitable result of a sense of failure in the inner life of a woman is an urgent desire for power. I believe that to be the reason why women missionaries—and indeed those at home, too—so often lose that integral quality of Christ-likeness, humility, and become so hard and dominating and so rabid about their work."

We had lecturers from outside, including Rev F W Dillistone, as well as the resident Miss Gray who lectured on the Bible, and Eveline Holmes who was in charge of the practical work we were all required to do. As I was a Guider I was given the job of captaining a Guide Company in the Victoria Docks area, which was quite an experience. This included visiting some of the homes of the Guides and sometimes enduring cups of tea which had been stewing on the hob, with sweet condensed milk—horrible!

After the first term at Kennaway, Miss Bothamley, who was the housekeeper, took three of us, Joan Cox, Laeta Marriott and myself to Cromer by car for the Cromer Convention at which Canon Raven was the chief speaker. We stayed at a Guest House on the sea front. Whilst we were there we visited Florence Allshorn at her cottage near Cromer. During this vacation I also went for a holiday to Cornwall with Joan Cox and her family. Florence was staying not far away at Mousehole and invited Joan and me over for the day. We had met unexpectedly whilst paddling!

On returning to Kennaway for the autumn term I was elected sacristan and was shown my duties by Elizabeth Rose fiancee of Peter Bostock who later became Provost of Nairobi Cathedral. As sacristan I had to be responsible for the cleanliness and order of the chapel, to keep the one arrangement of flowers fresh and attractive, and to prepare the vessels, bread and wine for Holy Communion. I enjoyed this work and it was a good preparation for my job the following term which was that of Prayer Secretary. I remember preparing with great pains a decorated poster for chapel to be used by students volunteering to lead morning and evening prayers and any other arranged services. These included the intercession service for missionaries every Sunday morning. On Sunday afternoons all students and staff met in the Common Room to hear read letters from former students working abroad. My natural diffidence and shyness had to be kept in check when meeting and thanking visiting speakers and preachers, and it was good experience.

The following term, January 1938, my friend Joan Cox was elected Senior Student and she asked me to be her deputy. It was just as well that I had this experience because at the end of that term I was elected Senior Student for the next term, which would be our first at the new college, Foxbury, Chiselhurst, Kent, a charming house with beautiful grounds and a rose garden.

During the summer Joan Cox, Marjorie Morton and myself lived at Foxbury for most of the vacation with Florence, Miss Bothamley and Eve Holmes, preparing the house for the great invasion of 48 students in October. We cleaned, arranged rooms, made curtains, shopped for items like lamp shades, had our meals together and generally enjoyed ourselves. We took time off to visit our homes and take any holidays which had been arranged. The rooms were allotted, the staff given the first choice, and I chose the room which was to be the Senior Student's. The house was full when term started in October, so full that Joan and Marjorie who were sailing at the end of the month had to sleep in a cubby hole off the Common Room. We all had jobs on rotas, I don't remember any staff engaged for the running of the house except Lily Hawksworth in the kitchen. She had been in Florence's Bible Class at Sheffield Cathedral years before. I asked Mary Miles to be my deputy.

As Senior Student I visited Florence in her study every morning to receive orders for the day and to report. She knew the background, history, record, ability and temperament of each student. Much could be said of Florence's teaching and her methods of training, and this has been written about in the book by J H Oldham, *Florence Allshorn and the Story of St Julian's*. For me it was a never to be forgotten period of my life, of development, widening horizons and inspiration.

The period spent in training was very important in forming lasting friendships which lasted over long periods during which the friends did not see each other. When Don returned to England and saw Joan Cox again in 1945, she commented on how easy it was to start again from where they had left off, after seven years apart. When she was in South Africa she was particularly pleased to meet other missionaries who had been in training with her, and in later life she still had a body of friends of whom she used to say, "She was in training with me."

At the end of 1938 I had my final interviews, said farewell to my mother, father, family and friends and sailed for Nigeria on 29th January 1939.

**High jinks during training.
Don is the central figure**

Part 2.

Rex Wyatt

1912 – 1939

Alfred Ernest Wyatt was born on 21 March 1912, at 3 Alfred Gardens near the centre of Southall in Middlesex. His mother was Louisa Nellie Wyatt, formerly Tovey, and his father, who registered the birth on 2 April, was Joseph Henry Wyatt. From my teens, when my grandfather had outlived two wives, I remember him as a surly old man with an aggressively protruding lower lip. Photographs of him in middle age show him as not much different. He had a habit of drinking tea from his saucer with a slurping noise which I rather admired. He also used to drink a sweet British wine, until his doctor told him to switch to Guinness. When my father came to visit him he would always give him a game of backgammon, which my father would always lose. At the time of the birth of Rex, his third child, he was an electric tram conductor, aged 30. During the first World War he served as a seaman in the Royal Navy, and, according to family tales, saw action in the Mediterranean, so he would probably have been away from home for most of the time until Rex was seven. In a letter written in 1945, Rex remarked to Don, who had not yet met his father, that "I am afraid Dad is very touchy and has to be humoured a bit."

There is little information on Rex's upbringing. He had an older brother, who died in childhood, and an older sister, Alice, who married and lived in Southall for most of her life. Although she lived within a mile or so of her father, she never saw him in the later part of his life, until just before his death, because he had greatly offended her husband, Stan Prickett. Rex's father and sister always called him "Alf." He never told me how he acquired the nickname of Rex, by which everyone else knew him for as long as I can remember. The earliest correspondence between Don and Rex hints that it may have been a contraction of Johannes Rex, with reference to A A Milne's rhyme "King John was not a good man". At some point his mother died, and his father re-married. I have a vague memory of the step-mother, spreading margarine impressively thickly.

Rex went to Southall County School from 1923 to 1928. According to his school reports he did well in mathematical subjects and had inconsistent successes in others. The final report said "Excellent work: must aim at Honours." His own skeletal statement of his "Personal History" says that he passed the London University Matriculation in 1928. In a letter written in 1945 he said, "I am prejudiced against private schools because in the end they are money-making concerns, my views are influenced perhaps because I had the benefit (?) of State education only."

In September of that year, the Rev A E d'Albertanson, of 30 Greenford Avenue, Southall, wrote him a testimonial which runs: "I have very great pleasure in bearing testimony to the good character and ability of Mr Alfred Ernest Wyatt, now living with his parents at 3 Alfred Gardens, Southall. I believe him to be exceptionally steady and reliable & can with much confidence recommend him for any appointment where integrity, industry & quiet gentlemanly conduct are of consequence." The word "integrity" was prominently mentioned in an address at his funeral service, and provides a theme running through his life.

Between 1928 and 1935 he held various clerical posts, in December 1930 he passed the Intermediate Examination of the Institute of Cost and Works Accountants, and at one stage he was a statistician for the Sperry Gyroscopic Co. Ltd. A few photographs from this period show a fresh-faced young man in what appear slightly awkward poses. He was very short and slim, and the photographs, being monochrome, do not show his bright red hair, which was accompanied by a pale skin with freckles. It is probable that all his life he had a tendency to seriousness and an occasionally explosive temper. He was accepted by the Church Missionary Society in November 1935, and on 19 February 1936 he was sailing from Liverpool, having been appointed as Assistant Manager (one of several) and Accountant of the Church Missionary Society's Bookshop in Lagos. There is no information in his papers on what brought him to this move away from suburban West London at the age of 23. He must have been active in his local church, and not only active, but taking every opportunity to learn about his faith, because within three months of reaching Nigeria he was licensed as a Lay Reader in the Diocese of Lagos.

On 19 February 1945 he wrote about the journey to Don:

"Nine years ago today I set sail from England for the first time; it was a miserable dull day on Merseyside and it was difficult to tell where the smoke ended and the cloud began. It was not a very inspiring beginning to my missionary career and the clouds have appeared again more than once since then. David Lomas was my cabin mate and he proved to be an indifferent sailor, particularly when we were approaching Madeira. My first glimpse of Africa was through a port-hole at Bathurst and as it was very early in the morning it was impossible to see anything clearly. Two events stand out; the first, coming up on deck after an evening service to see the lights of Madeira twinkling gaily; the second, coming into the lagoon at Lagos. Of

Freetown I have only a vague impression but I do remember the hills there."

He says nothing about the transition in 14 days from an English winter to the heat of Lagos, nothing about adapting to a different culture, a different daily rhythm, new responsibilities, new colleagues, new servants. He says nothing because all this would have been an experience similar to Don's. And whereas Rex would have been part of a community of British Christians, committed men and women with a strong belief that they were doing God's work, Don, three years later, went into a far more isolated situation.

As his later letters show, Rex fitted into a pattern of work, church services, prayer meetings, helping other CMS people, mutual entertainment, and tennis. It is unlikely that he played tennis before he went to Nigeria, but it was a staple of his social life there. Other missionaries would be weighing him up and assessing him, just as he would in future years be weighing up and assessing the latest newcomers, and wondering whether they would last long. More information on missionary life in Lagos comes from the letters he wrote to Don in 1944/45 and 1950/51, and the subject is dealt with more fully in section 5.

Rex arrived in Lagos on 5 March 1936 and was in leave in England during 1938, spending six summer months there and arriving and departing through Dover. The other information on this leave is scant. In a letter written in 1945 he said:

"I am not keen on Barry as a boy's name; it is the name of a small Welsh port and I was not greatly impressed by my only visit there in 1938."

This might tie in with a booklet he had retained on the Cardiff celebrations of the fourth centenary of the English Bible 18 June to 2 July 1938. Either he or his future wife kept a copy of the Order of Service for the London diocesan missionary festival's service at St Paul's Cathedral on Monday 23 May 1938

**Rex, date unknown—Don first fell in love
with his bright red hair**

Part 3.
Nigeria
1938 – 1941

Don's narrative resumes, interspersed with extracts from the first set of her surviving correspondence.

At the end of 1938 I had my final interviews, said farewell to my mother, father, family and friends and sailed for Nigeria on 29th January 1939. My cabin mate was Beryl Pring, who also came from Croydon. She knew the ropes as she had already spent one tour in Nigeria. After an uneventful voyage apart from being very seasick we arrived in Lagos, where I spent two nights in the Bishop's house. Beryl went up country to Kudeti and I boarded the boat Kalabar which took me to Port Harcourt. There was no one to meet me and I spent an anxious time wondering if I would ever get off the boat. However, the manager of Port Harcourt CMS Bookshop arrived eventually and took me to his house where I was given a meal quite alone, as Tom and Margaret Collins had been invited out. Not the best way of being introduced to a new country!

The next day I was put on a train to Aba about 40 miles away where I was met by Miss Winifred Yeatman (Yeatie) and taken to the Bride School, Abayi Umuochan. This was intended for girls 14-18 years old who were engaged to be married, and paid for by fathers or intended husbands to be taught housecraft, cooking, the three R's, dressmaking and child care. The buildings were primitive. Yeatie and I lived in a cement two bedroom bungalow with corrugated iron roof. The girls' dormitories and school-room were of red mud with corrugated iron roofs. The girls slept on simple beds with wooden slats and no mattresses. There was no tap water—each morning and evening the girls with debis (petrol tins) on their heads filed down to the river to collect water, which in the case of staff was boiled and filtered.

The girls' meals were cooked in the open under a rough shelter, the staff's on a woodburning stove in a primitive kitchen. We had a fridge run on paraffin.

I have very mixed feelings about my time at Abayi-Umuochan. Of course I had to teach in English and very few of the girls had a good command of that language. At the same time I was learning Ibo, the language of most of the girls, so we were learning from each other. The girls were very anxious to learn, and especially enjoyed learning to speak English and the dressmaking lessons. The creations we made were praised by the Government Inspector of Schools, Miss Gladys Plummer. I had only had the experience of making my own clothes, never having been to classes, but the girls were willing and able pupils and were delighted with the results of the lessons.

On the other hand I was very saddened by my Principal's treatment of the girls, resorting to harsh words and sometimes physical punishment for wrong doing. Miss Yeatman had been in Nigeria a number of years and had become very deaf as a result of taking quinine to ward off malaria. She was often unwell and her temper suffered. I was often on edge because of her treatment of the girls, the young teachers and other Africans.

By the time that Don started writing to Rex in September 1940, Winifred Yeatman had left and been replaced by Miss Dorothy Brooker, who had been working in Owerri province, apparently in a similarly isolated situation.

> In school holidays I sometimes stayed at St Monica's school, Onitsha, where Janet Clarke was Principal.
>
> It had been the rule for missionaries to go home every 18 months because of the climate, but the war came and CMS asked us to stay another year. So we were given local leave and I went by rail to a guest house run by the Sudan Interior Mission at Miango, 20 miles from Jos in Northern Nigeria. Here I met Rex Wyatt on leave from the CMS Bookshop, Lagos, and we walked and played tennis together, being the only guests in the house. When we parted we had promised to write to one another and I well remember Rex's first letter which began "Dear Don Parker".

Of this correspondence one letter from Rex survives, but there is a complete sequence of letters from Don. The letter from Rex is typed on Basildon Bond paper and is given nearly in full.

C.M.S. Bookshop, P.O.Box 174, Lagos.

Sept.2nd.1940.

Dear Don Parker,

I hope that you reached Aba safely after a comfortable journey. I was not very lucky, from Kaduna I shared a compartment with a Syrian who cleared his throat by day and snored by night, a peculiar smell in the compartment was probably due to the fact that he wore no shoes most of the time.

Under separate cover you should receive a parcel of books Dorothy Sayers, A.A.Milne and gramophone catalogues. The next parcel should include A New Approach to the Old Testament, Chesterton's St.Francis, Grey's Charm of Birds, Columbia Popular Standard Cat. I have looked up your order for Oxford Readers and I find that It was dealt with by Farmer, your letter was signed Edith V. Parker; we still owe you 9 Book 1, do you still require these?

Someone at Miango mentioned a book, W*ho Moved the Stone*, I cannot remember who it was but I understand that it is a book well worth reading. Have you any information about it Please?

Capital letters keep on creeping in where they are not required, I suppose that the fault is my own but it is most annoying. You will have noticed that this letter is addressed in accordance with one of your signatures, I hope that this is in order. In any case Why Don? I have not seen Miss Potts yet but expect to do so before the day is out, I will then deliver your messages.

I have arrived in time to be mixed up in a first class palaver, it may blow over or it may be a matter for getting the gloves on; if there is a scrap I will be in it. This letter is a peculiar mixture of business, books etc.

I hope that are all well [sic] at Aba and that the weather is not too bad. Are all of the pupils Behaving themselves?

[Paragraph about the price of HMV records]

I would like to finish up with a joke but I cannot think of one on the spur of the moment. Here is a quotation in-stead [sic] from an English business letter –CENSORED– I think that I had better leave it out.

Instead of using the signature Johannes R I will just use the Rex as the former is rather clumsy.

All the best,

Yours sincerely,
Rex
A.E.Wyatt

Do you think my typing is as good as my salesmanship?

In reply to the enquiry about the journey, Don wrote (10 September 1940):

....The journey from Jos was quite pleasant except for the heat which seemed to increase with every mile–I was more fortunate than you–had a compartment to myself all the way. I had an enjoyable weekend at Iyi Enu Hospital with a medical exam. thrown in, and travelled by lorry to Aba on Monday. Since then I have been immersed in all the work of a new term. 47 hefty young wenches have arrived in the best of spirits, which means plenty of noise.

.....I am, O Sire,

Yours sincerely,

Don

The letters give some insight into life at the Bride School. On 29 September she wrote:

A.A. Milne cheered many a lonely meal. Dorothy Brooker has been travelling for a fortnight and I have been alone. She is going off for a longer tour at the end of next week....

At the moment the work here is demanding a lot of attention because it's still in the building up stage, and I find that being on top of the girls & the buildings gets on top of me sometimes. But books & the gramaphone [sic] help considerably....

On 11 October, when Dorothy Brooker was away again, she wrote:

Life is very queer these days; things haven't been going very smoothly. Our Certificated Teacher who promised to be such a help when she first came, has been giving me a lot of trouble. A boarding school post does involve a lot more work for teachers & they know that when they agree to come. This teacher's school work is good, but she has not been willing to enter into the general life of the school & wants so much free time. She does such funny things too. The other morning I was awakened at 4.15 by a gramaphone playing jazz!. Things came to a head yesterday & we had a 'few words'; she seems quite different to-day & I hope it will continue—she's such a creature of moods. It's most disturbing. Dorothy is keen for us to have someone else. I think perhaps the right thing to do would be to keep her here & fight the thing out—trying to show her where she fails & saving her from herself. She's got good stuff in her but has been 'difficult' wherever she has been. It would mean sticking at it and sticking at it & I don't know if I'm strong enough to do it. But if I let her go I shall feel it is failure on my part, because she is still likely to be 'diffi-

28

cult' wherever she goes & after all she'll still be in
C.M.S.....I expect you have enough of your own
palavers....

Now I have to try & entertain the teachers. They
are coming to tea, & the junior ones are very shy.

On 13 November she was telling Rex:

Miss Plummer is coming here next Thursday to
inspect the school & examine girls for Certificate of
Merit. We want to go into the question of having
Standard VI here, with her, as the need has arisen in
the last year....

The Medical Board has recommended that I go
home in February.... Surely things at home will be
quieter by then.....

The crowd came last night & we had quite an
amusing time—two dignitaries & five priests—not a lay-
man among them. I think the Bishop is rather suspi-
cious of my dealing with the girls. We have two girls
who have recently broken their engagement. Both of
the men are teachers & the cases have been brought to
the Bishop's notice. He seems to think the girl should
have no say in the matter.

Writing on 3 December, she gives details of a weekend
with other missionaries at Ebu Owerri., when there was a
Prayer Meeting and a discussion on Evangelism:

Our discussion led us to the fact that the missionary's
quality of life & his relationship with fellow missionaries are of supreme importance. The younger women
missionaries on this side feel rather strongly about
these things. Most of us have been influenced by Miss
Allshorn's views on these subjects....

Don's autobiographical memoir continues:

The Christmas following, it was necessary to visit a dentist and as I had been invited to spend Christmas with John and Nora Lewis, who were friends of Rex's, I travelled to Lagos by lorry, staying at friends two nights on the way. Travelling by lorry was a great experience. A white person sat in the front seat by the driver with possibly two or three other Africans. The back was filled to overflowing with Africans and their luggage, which included cooking pots and household goods, and any produce and animals the driver had undertaken to deliver. At stopping places the noise was terrific, with the alighting of people and goods and the boarding of other people and goods, the loud greeting of friends and the laughter always noisy. My first night was with Bishop and Mrs Melville Jones who had retired from Lagos up country. *[On the return journey, Bishop Jones came part of the way from Lagos with her. She thought he had a slight cold, but he died within a few days.]*

The next day I travelled on by lorry to Akure where J. Mars and Dinah Hart ran a bride school. I stayed with them and learnt the story of the Christmas puddings they had made using 6lb of mixed spice and how they had realised their mistake and washed all the spice from the other ingredients and started again. When I told this story in Lagos, John Lewis sent a telegram to Akure ordering "6 laundered puddings" and 6 Akure Cookery Books, which J and Dinah had produced. This story caused much amusement in the Yoruba Mission for many months.

The visit to Lagos, though primarily intended for visits to the dentist, was not unmixed with pleasure, because by this time Rex and I had realised that our relationship was something different from friendship. By

30

the time I was due to return to Abayi-Umuochan we had become engaged. John and Nora Lewis were very co-operative in helping us to see one another.

On her way back, while waiting for a lorry at Benin, she wrote a brief note in pencil to Rex, which could be taken back to Lagos for her by the Paynes, who were going that way. She had left some things behind and says that she must have been "quite dithering". The next letter starts "My Dearest" instead of "Dear Rex", and ends "My love always" It was written from Iji Enu on 4 January 1941.

The journey from Lagos has been made quite exciting with congratulations and good wishes all along the way..... It's all very thrilling, darling, & I'm going to find it difficult to settle down to work; but it has to be done so perhaps it won't be so difficult. Dr McKebaie [?] is teasing me because I don't seem to know much about what is happening in Lagos from a military point of view & keeps asking questions I can't answer satisfactorily.

The following extracts from letters written in January provide hints and suggestions about the sort life she was leading, and her relationships with different colleagues. The salutations vary, but eventually settle down to "My dearest John Rex".

...It was lovely to see your letter dated 2nd sitting right on top of the pile awaiting me yesterday. I arrived at 3 o'clock after 7 ½ hours on a lorry. The lorries on this side are not nearly so satisfactory in speed & efficiency as on your side. It is only 100 miles from Onitsha to Aba, & was the worst part of the journey.

I believe I told you in my last letter that I was waiting until Tuesday to travel to Aba in order to be able
to see the Archdeacon when he called at Iyi Enu on his
way from Enugu. He had already heard the news at
Oji River when he arrived & said it was a great shock.
He was very nice about it really, & after some discussion he decided that I ought to try & go in March if
possible, but it depended finally upon what Dorothy &
I could arrange between us. There was the question of
Dorothy's Miango holiday, her travelling job, & the
handing over of the school.

Dorothy's reception of the news was the first
damper on my joy.... We have talked about when it
will be most convenient for me to go & have finally
decided that Dorothy will go to Miango immediately
after Conference & return on the 22nd March. It will
not be necessary for me to wait till the end of term
which is April 17th, but we shall need a few days in
which to hand over.

I had a bad few minutes with [Dorothy] the other
morning when she raised the subject of our engagement, but very soon after she came to me & apolo-
gised. The trouble is that she doesn't want to do
school work again & is afraid she may have to if a successor to me isn't found, & she doesn't want to live
with anyone else.

14.1.41 You dearest, darling man—I love you, love
you, love you more than ever for your last letter which
arrived this morning. It's the one telling me all about
the Conference & I'm so happy because of the tone of
it (the letter). I wish you were here & I would hug you.
If you had been here this morning & could have seen

my face, it was smiling all over—I could feel it. It isn't
the resolution of the Conference, tho' I am pleased
about that. It's because you had the right attitude in
the event of a refusal. Of course we wouldn't have
been happy if we had got an earlier marriage thro' trying to force the Mission's hand. And I'm glad you
wouldn't have used the threat of resignation. You must
have had a bad time, darling, but all our difficulties
can be halved now, because they are shared. There
may be more ahead, as you say, but <u>we</u> will meet
them.....

You ask me to tell you something more of the
Niger—I don't know where to begin. Perhaps I had
better start with the Delta, which is the part South of
Owerri & includes Bonny, Okrika, Brass & all the
Creek country, where all the pastors & catechists are
very fat because they almost live in canoes. Dorothy &
I are the only two C.M.S. European missionaries
working in the Niger Delta Pastorate with the excep-
tion of the Bookshop Staff (Mr & Mrs Collins, Mr &
Mrs Pearman & Mr O'Neill) & the Bishop when there
is one. For many years the N.D.P. refused to have
C.M.S. missionaries—they thought they could carry
on better by themselves & formed their own N.D.P.
Comparatively recently they realised that their
Church was very slack & asked C.M.S. for missionaries. The standards are still very low compared with the
Onitsha Archdeaconry, & Bishop Onyeabo & the really keen pastors find it really hard work trying to raise
them. They get little or no backing from the real Delta-
ites. We find the girls from the south, usually, more
difficult than those from the north.

This has been a busy day. The four new teachers
arrived yesterday & to-day, & the first impressions are

good ones. Loving you makes me more loving to other people & there has been an absence of strain & irritation these days since I returned, though I have been very busy & that's the way the Devil usually gets at me..... The girls return tomorrow–by lorry, train & bicycle. The new dormitory of mud & mats is still not quite finished–it has been hanging about for nearly 10 months when it was promised in a month! The girls are going into it tomorrow.

There never was such a hive of industry as this school the last few days, except perhaps sometimes the Lagos Bookshop office! There were many things to be done to get ship-shape. Most of our buildings are mud & mat roofs, & there is plenty of mud rubbing to be done. The girls & the teachers set to with a will. I had a talk with the teachers yesterday & all seem to have a nice attitude to the job. Now I am relaxing after spending most of the morning helping them with lessons....

Sundays in a boarding school are difficult to cater for. We try to avoid too much Churchgoing and meetings, but these girls do need organised occupation–they never think of trying to read a book, except the Bible. I am not yet satisfied with our programme, tho' it has been changed several times.

When the engagement ring arrived, she wrote:

I think the sight of it reminded Dorothy of our coming parting, & at tea time she said some rather horrid things. I just couldn't bear it & had a good weep privately. Poor Dorothy, it wasn't her real self at all. She has been having fever at nights & not sleeping. She retired to bed after tea. When I went to say "goodnight", she asked my forgiveness & broke down entirely. She said the fact that we were not going to live together much longer had been a great blow to her, & that the year we had lived together had been the happiest time of her life. Can you imagine it? She was brought up in a very sheltered home & is very repressed in her emotions. I feel so sorry for her. She has lived alone out here for nearly 13 years & now that she has settled down happily with someone it must be a blow to her. I will continue to give her my love, as you say, bless you.

In the same letter she worried about the prospect of separation after marriage because of a "ban on wives". Was there any possibility she could help maintain an "essential service"? Would secretarial work count?

Towards the end of January she became ill. The autobiographical memoir says:

> Soon after I returned to Abayi-Umuochan, the tummy trouble I had been having was diagnosed as amoebic dysentery and also malaria. When I became really ill I was taken on a mattress in the school truck to Port Harcourt Hospital where I underwent some horrible treatment which included the doctor sticking a 20 cc syringe into my tummy. However, I recovered and returned to the school.

There were in fact two episodes of illness, with a period of remission in between. During the period she was at the Niger Mission's Conference, and she was writing letters continuously throughout. Rex was on tour at the time, and at least one letter was sent to Ibadan.

I have just ordered 50 copies of the Church Hymnary as my parting gift to the school. Dorothy has begged me to break the news of my departure gently to the girls….. They have all noticed my ring, of course, & Dorothy is afraid the wearing of rings may become a fashion in the school. We try to discourage the wearing of "jewellery".

I am glad you have gained 2 lbs since the 11th. Keep it up. Perhaps I had better give an account of myself in the approved style. Tennis–nil. Bathing–nil. Drinking–mainly milk, ovlatine, orange juice neat. Eating–steamed fist, brains, light cheese dishes, no vegetables except potato. Reading–erratic. Working– almost nil, Resting–more than I like. Spirits–(not drinking) good. Loving–I find it hard to express the quantity & intensity for one person–my John Rex.

––––––––––––––––––––

We have to-day received Plum's report of the School & it really is a good one. She makes such comments as "the buildings have been improved," "domestic science very satisfactory," "Needlework was good, and dressmaking extremely good. The dresses made by the girls, under the Principal's direction, were well above the average in style, fit & finish," "On the literary side work is satisfactory" "Books neatly kept." "English in upper groups is very good." "Singing has been well taught."

… Think of me at the Conference getting my leg pulled–I know some of those wretched Onitsha men.

––––––––––––––––––––

I am sitting facing St Monica's gorgeous view: there's a lovely Flame of the Forest tree in full bloom, and an Indian Laburnum in the foreground. It's such a joy to be here after dull, flat, uninteresting Aba….

Janet C. …. Can't quite get over her disappointment that I am engaged, mainly because all the married people she has known have had the fine edge of their spirituality worn off after marriage....

I'm very glad I didn't go into Onitsha on Saturday. The Education Committee sat from 9 till 2.30, and the Women's Work Meeting from 4 till 6.30. This is Quiet Day & I shall probably go in for this evening's service. Tomorrow we are discussing "Evangelism" in groups. Each group (3) is discussing a different aspect of Evangelism & will have a Chairman & and an Opener. I am in the Group to discuss Evangelism in Training, i.e. schools, Colleges, Class meetings, etc. Janet Clarke is the Opener & Charles Forster Chairman......

I really think that horrible A.D. bug has been successfully dealt with & I want to get my full strength back so that I can get on with the job.

___

Conference has been going well, especially to-day. Yesterday (Monday) we discussed Evangelism in Groups.... There were two distinct schools of thought in our group which made discussion difficult—those of us who are dissatisfied with the present superficial evangelism in most of our places of learning, and those who are more or less content to go on [as] they have been going on. Actually it was mainly the women in the first group & the men in the second. Janet suggested that certain people in the Mission, as soon as possible, should be free to do direct evangelism only. Such people who felt called to this work would be freed from the hampering routine of an institution, the problem of time, and live in a bush place as simply as possible with Africans whom the Europeans would train to be spiritual leaders. Rather on the lines of a Franciscan community. This place could also be used as a Retreat & for language when recruits first came

37

out. Of course, the necessary work of indirect Evangelism would still go on in schools & colleges. At the moment there are no people doing direct evangelistic work.

To-day the findings of all the groups were present & a summary made followed by further general discussion. David Money made a suggestion very much on the lines of Janet's, arising out of the great need which people in the Worship group felt for Retreats. He suggested that we should start with only one man who knew the language & felt that nobody would be better than Archdeacon Wilcock...

The marvellous thing is that Freddie [Wilcock] has had the great need of a Diocesan Missioner on his heart for a long time & later in the Conference it was to come up for discussion.

When all the Evangelism discussion was finished the Bishop thought the time had come to introduce the subject of a Missioner. Freddie spoke of what he had in mind—that the man should live in a central place—not a town, to which recruits could go for language, missionaries for Retreats & from which he would conduct his evangelistic campaigns. He offered himself for the work. Freddie went out while we discussed the matter, but it was very evident that the whole thing was a movement of the Spirit & we were unanimous in our decision that such a thing should happen.

Those of us who have been dissatisfied with the lack of spirituality in the Church & the great emphasis on numbers were thrilled with this new attitude.

Everybody is agreed that Conference this year was grand. I believe I told you about the appointment of a Diocesan Missioner. You mustn't say a word about our Bookshop discussion, your end. When the subject came up for discussion it was introduced by George Cockin, one of our young educationists, in a masterly speech. I wish I could remember it. He made me feel that the ideal function of the Bookshop could be a thrilling thing, not just a means of providing money to help carry on the institutions of the Mission, but an evangelistic agency in itself.

Tom Collins had no real answer to the challenge re prices, & adjustment is going to be made in that direction. The Bishop read out a long list of books etc, comparing Lagos & our prices in which ours showed up very badly. One outcome of the very long discussion in which people spoke quite freely, is that the Bookshop Committee is to be supplemented by 4 members, 3 of them educationists to advise re the choice of books for stock.

My friends are all keen that you & I should come over this side & be the ones to make our Bookshop into a real evangelistic agency, perhaps travelling from one shop to another, helping the clerks to display the right kinds of books, reading new books which come on the market. It would be an entirely new kind of Bookshop job, & exists only at the moment in the minds of about 6 of my women friends, but I must say it appeals to me. Another reason for wishing us to come this side is that they think we could help in establishing a right relationship between the unmarried men & women of this Mission. At the moment there could easily be fellowship between them if it weren't for the gossip among a few when a fellow &

girl are even seen talking together. Janet & others think that we (you & I) would be able to invite them to our home where they could meet in the right atmosphere.

I don't know what you think of our transferring you (in thought) to the Niger Mission, but if the Lagos Bookshop can't afford a married couple, there might be a chance of it, as our people are so keen on this new Bookshop idea.

Dorothy went off to Zaria yesterday & Kaye Simmons came to keep me company. [She was still weak and wrote that] The head teacher is rising to the occasion well.

I think when Janet talked about "the fine edge of spirituality being worn off in married people she had known, was that often she has seen a really keen girl doing a fine piece of work, drop back into a second best after marriage. But I do agree with you that married life provides a new sphere of action in Christian living, & in some cases partnership means greater Christian influence, or influence in a wider circle. Also, we have left out one important point—that if we believe God is directing our lives (& I assume you have prayed about your future as I have), then surely He has brought us together.

Your letter of the 17th from Akure arrived Saturday morning when I was perspiring freely under the bedclothes with a sharp attack of fever. I had had two days without pain & then this came. Consequently Kaye wouldn't go to Ebu for the weekend, but stayed to nurse me. Darling, you will think you are engaged to a crock, but I can assure you that this is the longest bout of ill health I have ever had. When I had appendicectomy [sic] I was in bed for a fortnight, at home recuperating for a fortnight, & then back at Weybridge Hospital on full nursing duties, which is good going.....

Do you know any friendly person at Oshogbo who would give me a bath & a meal before travelling on the night train to Lagos? If not, do you think the Bookshop clerk would oblige? I think there are about 2 hours between the arrival of the lorry at Oshogbo & the departure of the train for Lagos. If all goes well, & you agree, I think I will ask for permission to leave here on the 18th March , as Mr Baxter of U.A.C. Motors travels to Onitsha on that day & he will take me. I can get to Benin the same night, travel to Akure or Oshogbo on the 19th, & arrive on the morning of the 20th or 21st at Lagos. Does the night train go from Oshogbo to Lagos every night or every other night?...

Did the Bookshop opening go well? According to your description it should have been a most impressive ceremony....

Perhaps I'm a little critical when people talk about love—we had such good teaching on that subject from Miss Allshorn. We weren't allowed to talk idly & vaguely about love—we had to put into practice....

I shall be glad when you get back to Lagos because we can answer one another's letters quicker.

The next time she wrote it was to say that she would be going into Port Harcourt Hospital. Her subsequent letter, written from the European Hospital, gives a different account of the journey from the one in the autobiographical memoir, but presumably she was taken on a mattress in the school truck as far as the railway station.

I caught the 8 o'clock train this morning, which reached P. H. about 10. The Hospital ambulance was waiting for me—I felt quite a fraud being able to walk into it. .... Upon arrival I was greeted by two sisters, shown into a very pleasant room, & popped into bed. A cup of tea, followed by several questions on a slate, were the next items.... I wondered if you are my next of kin, but I suppose you aren't—yet. ..... Next came Dr Braithwaite. Do you know him, or have you heard of him? He talks all the time in short, jerky sentences. "Let's look at your teeth. Open your mouth. OPEN. Don't be afraid. H'm, quite a good set. Yes, quite good. You've lost a molar. Get down in the bed. Any pain? Ah, there it is. None there?" As a matter of fact I think he has put his finger on the trouble, quite literally. I couldn't quite catch what he said about the tender spot on my tummy, but it's evidently the after effects of A[moebic] D[ysentery].

.... And now to answer your very important question. "Are you still willing to become Mrs Bookshop in face of such a probable future?" Darling, you know that I am willing, & not only willing, but it is my heart's desire to become your wife whatever the future. And having said this I shall not make you unhappy by being dissatisfied when we are married—I shall be content & glad to help you in your work in any way I can. But I would like us to keep our dream in mind—I hear the doctor, & the nurse is pulling the screen ready for the injection.

It was given into my tummy & I hope it's the last. To continue. I would like us to keep our dream at the back of our mind, so that when & if the time comes we may be ready to do the dream job to the best of our ability. I am so glad to know that you have visualised a similar job to that which we dreamed of. It is some-

thing about which we can pray and plan together–
even if it never materialises–I am quite thrilled about
it.

Mrs Currie is going home to morrow & I shall be
the only patient with a doctor, two sisters, two nurses,
a dispenser & umpteen hospital staff to attend me, & all
for 5/- a day. The loneliest time is in the evenings.

I've just had rather a blow. One of the teachers has
come down by train to bring a telegram from Dorothy
saying she isn't returning to Abayi until Thursday
instead of Monday, and also to say that she (the
teacher) is going to Lagos to be a midwife. This was
in the wind before I came away & Bishop Onyeabo has
given her permission. She has been teaching Std IV &
it won't be easy to replace her. I'm sorry it has happened while both Dorothy & I are away. It will make
things more difficult for the Head teacher. I can't do
anything about it now I am here, but I wish it hadn't
happened. Of course, Dorothy doesn't know I am in
hospital...

You were a bit 'down in the dumps' when you
wrote from Abeokuta. I hope the Bookshop palaver
didn't turn out as bad as you expected. I know that
horrible feeling of sickness which comes with
palavers...

I couldn't help smiling when I read that the quality in me which first attracted you was the capacity for
standing on my own feet. Actually I am very uncertain
of myself & very shy, but 5 terms at Kennaway &
Foxbury cured me of many of the outward signs. In
my last term I was Senior Student, the first S.S. of
Foxbury & I just had to make myself do things which
would have seemed impossible two years before. And
you must remember that I had already been at

43

Miango nearly 5 weeks when you arrived & felt quite at home, in spite of new arrivals. I was probably more shy of you than anybody, because were so quiet! A large part of my life has been governed by my fears, & tho' some have been conquered others still have a strong hold over me. What a lot we shall learn together!

The Sister gave me permission to go out to tea yesterday at the Collins's, & afterwards Margaret took me for a run round P.H. in the car. This is only my third visit in 2 years & one of the others was to come here in November [??] 1939.

The next letter was written partly in the European Hospital and partly back at Aba.

I shall have a busy week handing over to the Head Teacher. It was decided at Standing Committee that she is to be Acting Principal until somebody comes to take my place. I think it is expecting a great deal of her, especially where the books & money are concerned. I expect Dorothy will keep an eye on her & the school.....

Dorothy was at the station to meet me yesterday & I was glad to be back.....

You mention the possibility of the Bookshop being unable to meet the extra fare if we went by Johnora's route to S.A. Surely the Niger Mission would pay my fare & not the Bookshop, as I have done a full tour in the Niger Mission; even if we were married first this should stand.

Today I have spent part of the time in school & part in the office clearing up odds & ends. The

44

accounts were in an awful muddle owing to my absence, but we have managed to settle them. Dearest, I shall let you do the housekeeping accounts – I'll try & manage the household staff if you will do that!

A few days ago the girls told Dorothy they wanted to have a group photograph taken to give to me. So yesterday we put on our best bibs & tuckers & tried to look beautiful. The girls were very funny – they unplaited their hair & tried to do it European fashion & they held flowers in their hands & looked soulful! This evening they asked Dorothy when they could some plays for me, so they are going to give me a good send off. I wish it were over.

…On Sunday I am to take the evening service & give my last message to the girls, a thing which I never find very easy – I am not a born speaker….

Don's autobiographical memoir says:

> There was no reason for Rex and me to delay our marriage as by this time we had both worked for 2½ years which was the CMS requirement for engaged couples, and we were both due for leave. My parents had cabled suggesting that we did not go home to Croydon to be married as they were practically living in an air raid shelter in the garden, so with seven other missionaries we were booked to go to South Africa for leave.

She and Rex had discussed various possibilities over a period of time, including going to Northern Nigeria ("the plateau"). They decided not to get married until they got to

South Africa – there is no knowing whether this was because of the advice of Dr Margaret Roseveare, repeated by other women doctors: "Don, <u>don't</u> rush the wedding too quickly. One just can't trust one's emotions out here, however genuine they may seem. Even a South African climate would have a balancing effect!"

Don went to Lagos to wait for a boat. With the uncertainty of wartime travel, one person she knew had missed a passage home because he was not on hand at the right time. Her luggage sent in advance to Lagos was 1 case of china & glass 1 case of books & gramaphone, 1 case of stores, 1 trunk containing clothing etc., 1 zinc lined case containing linen, pictures, etc., 1 folding table, 2 stools, 1 bicycle, 1 hat box, 1 camp bed, eleven packages in all.

> The opportunity for berths on a ship did not come for about seven weeks. In the meantime I was living at the CMS Girls' School House, Lagos, with Miss Grimwood (Grimmie), Nancy Wedmore and Irene Humphries who were on the staff. I filled my time by designing and making school uniform dresses in mauve cotton for the pupils. This pattern and colour were still in use when Hilary became a pupil about eight years later.

Rex and Don on their Wedding day.

Part 4.

South Africa and Lagos
1941-1943

Don's autobiographical memoir continues:

At last in June we embarked on the Sobieski, a
Polish vessel which had at one time been captured by
the Germans who had, it was said, had acid poured into
the engines so that she could not make good speed.
None of the stewards could speak English and they
seemed to be untrained. The voyage was uneventful
until we got into the Cape rollers in which we were
hove-to at Cape Town Harbour which was packed with
ships waiting to be unloaded. We spent one night being
flung from one side to the other. The furniture in the
lounge, including a grand piano, was flung through the
french windows on to the deck where a number of our
party had elected to sleep because it was so warm.
Crockery was thrown to the floor, the baths on legs
juddered across the floors of bathrooms, the noise
throughout the night was indescribable. In the calm-
ness of the next morning we walked from one end of
the ship to the other to see the night's damage. Cape
Town Harbour was choc a bloc with ships and because
we had to wait our turn we were short of food sup-
plies which had to be brought out to us by ship.
Eventually after four days we got ashore and were
met by the Rev A W Lasbrey, the brother of Bishop

Lasbrey (Bishop on the Niger), who had charge of five churches in the Cape Town area. He had arranged accommodation for the nine of us, and Rex and I were put in a small Cape Town hotel, in rooms next door to one another. Mr and Mrs Lasbrey undertook to arrange our wedding, even to supplying the wedding cake, and we were able to choose at which of his five churches we would have the marriage ceremony: Kenilworth Church, Wynberg, a small English looking church. At the ceremony and the reception in the Vicarage there were 14 CMS missionaries on leave in South Africa and members of the South Africa CMS. After the reception Mr and Mrs Lasbrey drove Rex and myself to a seaside cottage near Simonstown belonging to Mrs Lasbrey's father, stopping on the way for food. In the butcher's, to the amusement of the butcher, I asked Rex if he liked pork chops, giving away my lack of knowledge of his food preferences. We never forgot the kindness of Mr and Mrs Lasbrey at that time.

The nearest shops were at Simonstown, a naval base four miles away, and we had to show the permits with which we had been provided before we were allowed through the gates. After a very happy fortnight in the cottage we returned to Cape Town for a few days at the Andrew Murray Missionary Home before travelling up country by train to a farm in the Little Karroo. The journey from the town of George up to the Little Karroo was made on a single track rail with spectacular views on both sides of the train. Our destination was an ostrich farm at Oudtshoorn, owned by an Afrikaans farmer and his wife, who gave us enormous meals. One ostrich egg provided enough scrambled egg for twelve people. Very often as well as the meat dish there were as many as twelve vegetables to choose from, followed by a substantial sweet course.

Often there were twelve people around one big table. The farmer tapped on the table for silence to say grace, which for the benefit of the English people present he said in English, to the disgust of his anti-English sister, a lecturer at Stellenbosch University, who would immediately break into a rapid flow of Afrikaans.

The rainfall in the Little Karroo is very low and the farm land was divided by channels to make the most of the water supply. There was only one afternoon when it rained a little in the month we were there.

This time in South Africa was in lieu of our home leave, so we had time to stay longer. We rented a small bungalow on the island at Knysna, which John and Nora Lewis, also staying on the island, had found for us. This almost uninhabited island was not strictly an island as it was joined to the mainland by a causeway. Nora and John were expecting their first baby and very soon I became pregnant. The war was still on and there were no white children in Lagos and no medical facilities for pregnant women, so when John and Rex were due to return, Nora and John and Rex and I had to make the painful decision to separate for the time being, John and Rex returning to Lagos and Nora and I staying on the island.

It is from this period that there is another set of correspondence. Unfortunately there is, again, only one side to it, the letters from Don to Rex. Don wrote a daily instalment, and the letters were posted twice a week, so from 15 November 1941, the date of the first letter, to the last instalment on 23 February 1943 there is a mass of material, much of it the trivia of day to day living I do not propose to quote from the correspondence in detail, but to pick out themes of interest.

Airmail letters took about ten to 15 days. Even the cable which announced Rex's arrival in Lagos took 9 days to reach "the island", and as the ship itself had taken longer than expected Don had been worrying for some time. When a letter did not arrive as expected, it caused great distress. "I sat in the sun parlour & watched & when they came eagerly jumped up. Sure enough the boy had two a[ir] m[ail] envelopes. When I grabbed them & looked at the name they were both for Nora & not one for me. I nearly wept with disappointment. Then I went for a walk & found myself crying." One reason for the length of time was the censorship–Don comments occasionally that she hopes the censor is not bored. Only one letter of hers was censored, with a neat little hole cutting out the name or title of a person who had been on trial for some criminal offence, an event which had occasioned some disturbance in Knysna; whereas there was no censorship of a later mention of an explosion in an explosives factory. A consequence of the long time it took to get replies was that, although Don would consult Rex about her decisions, she usually had to make up her mind before she got an answer. Sometimes she would tell him to cable if he disagreed with what she was proposing, but sending several cables herself was not within her normal budget.

Managing on her limited means was a constant theme of her letters. Money was forwarded by an agent in Capetown, and whenever she had to ask him for more than her usual amount, she was very apologetic and defended it in detail.

A very short distance away on the island another Lagos wife, Sylvia Smithies, was also awaiting the birth of her first baby. The climate was perfect and the sea water warm for bathing. It was an ideal place for a holiday, especially as from time to time we had visits of friends from Nigeria also spending their leave in South Africa, among them J. Mars, Dinah Hart and Beryl Pring.

Nora's baby was overdue and Dr Langsmidt in Knysna decided she must have a caesarean section, and

51

she was delivered of a son - John. Sylvia Smithies had to be rushed into the Knysna Nursing Home for a very premature birth - a girl. It was thought that Sylvia had overdone swimming in the sea.

When my baby was nearly due I had a visit from Winifred Noordendorp who lived in Knysna and whose husband was away in the army, asking if I would join her and her adopted baby in her Knysna house. This would obviate the difficulty of transport to the mainland when my time was due. This I agreed to do, and left Nora and baby John in the care of our little helper. [Another reason for moving was that relationships had become rather difficult, but they continued on good terms and continued to see each other.]

Although the doctor had predicted that I would drop my baby in the street because I was so active, the birth proved to be abnormal too. I was in labour for five nights and four days, and the delivery was by forceps under an anaesthetic. However, all was well and I was able to cable Rex that his son was born. We had already decided that he should be called Martin. I received Rex's cable and several others.

I lived with Winifred Noordendorp for some months. We were very much aware of the anti-British feeling in the town especially among the members of the Dutch Reformed Church.

The anti-British feeling does not come over in the letters. What does come over is the resentment against the families evacuated from Malta and Egypt who had been placed in Knysna. The resentment was all the stronger because this influx of refugees exacerbated the wartime shortages. Apart from that, Don's comments on the war news show quite unrealistic hopes that the war might soon be over.

Among all the little details and difficulties of keeping going, making do and mending, together with gossip about people known and unknown to Rex, there is some mention of her devotional life, of which the following is perhaps the fullest example (in June after the birth of the baby):

"At the end of my last letter I said I was going to make a fresh start with my devotions, & since coming to bed I have read part of the chapter in John which contains our special text. Then I found in my Bible your notes of the sermon you preached on that text & I found some sentences very helpful–'Whatever the circumstances–the mark of peace in face of tribulation.' 'True peace is only to be found in (Jesus who has overcome the world)–God.' For the last week or so I have been very low & dispirited as you have probably gathered from my letters & found little things upset me so I know that I have been trying to live in my own strength instead of drawing strength from God. There are also accounts of the services she attended - more frequent once she had moved into Knysna - and the shortcomings or otherwise of the clergy.

The most important theme cropping up from time to time in this series of letters is the dilemma of what to do about children. There is no way of knowing what was discussed before Rex left. The first time it crops up in the letters is in February before the birth when Don writes:

"What about my leaving A.M. [Audrey/ Martin, depending on whether it is a girl or a boy] down here & coming to you for the rest of the tour? It would mean of course that we would have come down here for our next furlough to fetch A.M."

But then in March she was involved in a discussion about it while visiting the nursing home.

"Dr Langschmidt asked when Nora was going back to Nigeria & Sylvia told him June, & added that she supposed she, Sylvia, wouldn't be able to get a passage. Sister asked what she would do with her baby if she could go & she said leave it here. Then Dr Langschmidt said he'd never met such a lot of unloving mothers to leave their babies & go to their husbands. Sylvia said she would probably cry her eyes out if she did go. I felt like weeping then & there. It's very easy for people to talk when the problem has never arisen for them & it makes it so hard when people criticise & say that you don't care, when it must be like tearing yourself in half. I think for myself, when the time comes I must put aside my own wanting you, (& that's desperately enough) & try & decide whether you or A.M. needs me most."

At the beginning of April she writes:

"Now to answer your points about the possibility of my returning to Nigeria this tour. I think I mentioned it several times in certain letters because I was feeling rather envious of Nora, but lately I have been thinking about it in a more reasonable way. Of course I want to be with you as soon as I possibly can, but I do realise that if we have the gift of a child we must do the best we can for it, & I don't know that leaving a child in S.A. would be the best thing. When I see how desperately the Nordendorps would have loved a child of their own, & wouldn't even part with their adopted child, it makes me feel a worm to even contemplate leaving A.M. I agree with you that we cannot expect the Bookshop to foot the bill for a double journey for both of us, if I returned to Lagos as your wife & we wanted to come down here to fetch A.M. on our way home. On the other hand it would be, as you say, very difficult to be separated from you most of the time, & from A.M. all the time, if I did a job up country." Later that month, when she was in the nursing home expecting the birth, the question of Nora Lewis and her son came up again: "I did not know that Nora had sent a cable ~~saying~~ worded that she could not return yet owing to being unable to get suitable accommodation for young John. Actually that is not true as Mrs Judd was quite willing & even anxious to have him. After Nora had asked her to have him, & she had changed her mind about wanting to go back, she made the excuse that an elderly relation with cancer was living with the Judds (likely to live only about 2 months) altho' Mrs Judd said it would make no difference at all to John's being there. From what Nora told me it was her letter after he first "willing" cable telling John that she <u>wasn't</u> ~~able~~ very willing to return, and his reply influenced by Evelyn Dunn's opinion of her health, which made John suggest that she should not go back after all, as they could always make the baby the excuse. I can't understand why John was mystified by the "unable" cable, as it was his suggestion that she should remain & I think Nora sent it to satisfy C.W.W. However, it seems to be all settled now, unless Nora changes her mind again."

In the months after the birth, Don came round to the idea that the only way out of their dilemma was for her to return with Martin to Lagos. It appears that this idea challenged the conventional wisdom about the Lagos climate and conditions not being suitable for white children, and that Rex was strongly opposed to it for that reason. The long distance argument escalated into strong terms.

In September Don wrote:

"Why can't ~~I~~ we come to you early in 1943 and wait for you to have your leave…. If you come here for leave in June & are still against Martin's going to Lagos it ~~will~~ would mean that I would have to stay behind. Please don't ask me to do it, dearest, I can't. It is not reasonable to instance the Hobsons' baby– Babies get ill everywhere –Knysna included. You say that the housing situation makes it impossible for me to come to Lagos in the immediate future. If I had returned with you as everybody expected, we should have to be living somewhere, and since you wrote there is the possibility of a home in the Mission House as I have suggested in an earlier letter.

At one time I would have been scared to face the voyage with a baby, but as time has gone on & with some of the best years of our lives, & considering the present state of the world – I feel that I am prepared to live dangerously….. In spite of all you say (& Mr. Tommy for whose opinion I haven't much respect) I am still prepared & want to bring Martin to Lagos ~~for~~ after he is 6 months to await your furlough time, & to decide when that time comes where it will be spent. Or I will (reluctantly) wait for you here until June for your furlough, to return with you & Martin to Lagos. Call me coward if you will, <u>but I cannot face another tour, or part of a tour, in this country</u> away from relations & friends & with no home of my own.

Only to-day Sister said that Martin is such a strong child he would be all right in Lagos, and tho'

56

she may not know all there is to know about the climate, she does understand babies. If we decided to bring Martin to Lagos it would not be Mr. Tommy's or anyone else's responsibility. I should look after the child and I am prepared to take the responsibility. He is losing far more through not having a father in these early days, than he would lose in the way of health."

It is evident from other letters that Rex himself had no very high opinion of Mr Tommy (Mr Thompson, the Bookshop Manager) though the material does not make clear the reason for this. At this time, as is shown by the address quoted later, Mr Tommy and Rex were keeping the Bookshop going under very difficult circumstances, and this may have influenced Rex's attitude to having a small child around.

A month later she is apologising for the possibility of having given any hurt for anything she may have written in her letters, but a fortnight after that she has to write again in very unhappy language, of which the following is only a small sample:

"I am quite content to wait for you here if you are coming down in April, but to expect me to go to England with Martin when you return to Lagos is too much. You write as if getting home is the most important thing for me, but as I said in a previous letter, much as I want to go home it is of very little importance compared with being with you. Do you realise that if I go home when you return to Lagos for a 2 years' tour, (as you will not expect another short one after this short one) we by the time I see you again we shall have been married over 4 years or 50 months spend only 8½ or 9 months together, as you say that wives are not allowed to return? I think it is unfair and unnecessary. Such a plan had never entered my head, & I don't know how you could even consider it. (And I shall be 38.)" The topic continued from time to time.

On one occasion Don wrote:

"Your letter dated 26-29th Nov. came this morning & while I was very pleased to have it part of it upset me rather. You say, 'You write of it (Martin's return) as your one great hope, which seems to suggest that there is no room for an alternative" and almost in the next sentence you say, "I feel I would be doing wrong, committing sin, if I agreed to Martin coming to Lagos." I can see no room for an alternative in that statement – I can't think of anything more definite – it hardly indicates an open mind!"

Eventually it was agreed to drop the topic until they were able to discuss it face to face.

The account in the next paragraph of the memoir compresses and alters the sequence of events. Don had decided to go to a farm in the Western Cape as a break from her joint housekeeping arrangement with Winifred Noordendorp, and to meet Mary Miles. Before going she decided to stay there indefinitely, for a number of reasons, including the difficulty of rail travel. This was before she knew the date of Rex's return to South Africa. The episodes bring out the extent of Don's charm. She got help from all sorts of people, had no difficulty in extending stays, and was invited back when she left. People confided in her and she was consulted by Kaye Morris on personal and religious matters.

Martin thrived and when he was about six months having received news from Rex that he was to get compassionate leave after a 15 month tour, he and I travelled by train to Somerset West near Cape Town to stay on a farm, to be nearer Rex when he arrived in Cape Town. While I was there, Mary Miles who had been my Deputy when I was Senior Student at Foxbury came there for a holiday as she was also on leave. After a time when the farm was full of holiday guests I moved to be the only paying guest at a farm not far away. The farmer Redvers [Morris] and his wife Kaye had a son Roddy, 2½, and a three month old baby girl. It was quite obvious that all was not well with the baby, who was so different from big, bouncing Martin, and after a time Kaye told me she was seeking the advice of a specialist in Cape Town. We were all very sad when he told Kaye that the baby was a mongol.

On 24 January 1943 she summarised her life in Africa in a letter to Rex:

"Dearest, it is 4 years to-day since Beryl and I sailed for Nigeria. It was snowing and very cold. Now it is mid-summer & quite warm. What a lot has happened in those 4 years which little expected to happen. A black first year followed by a brighter 6 months, then a high-light when I met you followed by a period of growing happiness until you asked me to marry you. From that time on we were together until you sailed last November, except for the 2½ months at Aba when we wrote very happy letters, so you know the rest of the story. There have been times of very great joy and happiness, and some of sorrow and loneliness and pain, bodily and mentally, but your coming into my life has been the greatest and best thing which has happened to me. Now I am looking forward to our reunion—you are part of my life, and I shall be a whole personality when we are together."

When Martin was eleven months Rex arrived from Lagos. Kaye had managed to find a three room flat with no furniture at all, and she very nobly provided us with a bed and some other furniture. The idea was that Rex should have a short leave and return with Martin and me to Lagos, as by that time Europeans were bringing out their children rather than leave them in the air raids and food shortages at home. However, there seemed to be no way of travelling to Lagos. Eventually, after seven months we booked to travel by train to Luluabourg in the Belgian Congo and from there by plane to Lagos. How differently it turned out! After four days in the train we thankfully detrained at Victoria Falls where we were refreshed in the luxurious Victoria Falls Hotel for 24 hours and were able to see the Victoria Falls and walk in the Rain Forest. Unfortunately Martin was too young to remember this experience. We had another four days and nights in the train to Luluabourg which was a very small wretched town with one hotel, one shop and a railway station. As soon as possible Rex went to the Airways office to find out about our booked flight to Lagos, only to find that there were no air tickets for us. We discovered afterwards from people who had travelled on the same train that their travelling companions by name Wyatt-Tilby had said that they had not booked on the plane to Lagos but that they would be all right for a plane. They must have known that the Belgian Congo officials were at that time susceptible to bribes for they got their seats on the plane while we were left to languish in the one miserable hotel for a week. The food was unsuitable for Martin and he suffered from tummy trouble.

When it became clear that there would not be another plane for at least three weeks we decided to go by train to Port Francqui where we could get a river steamer to Leopoldville (now Kinshasa). It was another 18 hours in the train. When we went aboard a river steamer on the River Kasai we were allotted a very small cabin with two very narrow wall bunks and nowhere for Martin to sleep. We spent a very restless night trying not to smother Martin. The steamer was wood burning so every night it was tied up and huge logs thrown on board. That noise, the constant battle against mosquitoes (in spite of nets) and the rowdy parties held by the drunken Captain made sleep almost impossible. By the second night, though, a cot of a kind had been found for Martin. It was a wooden structure with a cloth bag hanging from it. We had to pad the bottom so that Martin could be on the top and not smother in the well. It was a terrible voyage, though we tried to make the best of it. The food was very fatty and unsuitable for a child. The drinking water was undrinkable and we used it for washing ourselves. We drank bottled mineral water. The baths were disgusting so we never had a bath.

When we arrived at Leopoldville and went into a Baptist Mission Guest House it was like heaven. We were told we would have to wait three weeks for a plane but it proved to be only a week. It was a very flimsy ramshackle machine and my first flight, so I was very nervous besides feeling ill. We made two stops, at Dambarene and Dowala I think. At one of them our plane was thought to be carrying an important personage, and a band was out to meet us. Each time we took off we wondered whether if the plane would make it.

It was a great relief to arrive at Lagos Airport where a kind Nigerian boy lifted Martin from the plane. After the time of greeting our friends and fellow workers we soon settled into a Bookshop house in Racecourse Road behind Broad Street, the main street in Lagos, and Rex returned to work at the CMS Bookshop. The war was still on and food and other prices had risen in our absence. Lagos was an army base and the sellers in the market and shops had taken advantage of the army presence to raise prices. However, there was no shortage of food and we experienced little of the privations of war, whilst my family at home were having a very uncomfortable, to say the least, time.

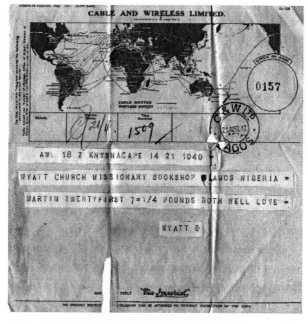

This cable arrived the same day it was sent, which did not always happen under wartime conditions

Part 5.

Nigeria

1943 -1951

In 1944 Don returned to England on her own, in the expectation of giving birth. Both sides of the resulting correspondence have survived. On Easter Day, 1 April 1945 Rex was writing:

"We have been married 3¾ years today, in another three months we shall have been married four years. So far we have enjoyed married life for twenty five months and the rest of the time has been spent in separation."

Don's memoir continues:

In 1944 I was pregnant again and was losing weight. The doctor advised me to go home for the birth, so Martin and I were fitted out with trousers for the voyage, having been told we would have to sleep in our clothes because of enemy submarines. We were given berths, along with a few other civilian passengers, on a troopship taking home military personnel. Martin and I shared a cabin with a missionary woman doctor who was badly seasick and kept to her bunk the whole of the voyage except when the ship was hove-to outside Gibraltar. The voyage was uneventful as far as Gibraltar, though the ship was crowded and the food indifferent, but it was wartime. At Gibraltar it was rumoured that the ship had been followed by submarines and so we were going to stay there for some days, which would include Christmas Day, so some of the women, including myself, were given permission to go ashore to buy presents for the children. So in this way I saw Gibraltar. But on Christmas morning we sailed again having been eight days at Gibraltar. The sea was very rough and I with my doctor cabin mate was very seasick. Martin was taken down to the dining room for Christmas dinner by kind friends who looked after him whilst I was laid low.

We arrived at blacked out Gourock, Scotland, late on New Year's Eve. We were going to stay with my sister Nora and her husband in Newcastle and the Disembarkation Officer said it would be impossible to find accommodation in Glasgow and it would be advisable to go on to Newcastle. We were taken to Glasgow Station by car where we boarded a train to Newcastle via Edinburgh. Martin had a terrible cold and was crying with cold or coughing, and I had luggage and a pram to cope with besides being very cold, so it was not the most happy of journeys. At Newcastle we had to wait a long time for a taxi and then shared one with several people for various destinations. Eventually we arrived about 2.30 a.m. and a very astonished Nora opened the door to us. Of course I had not been able to let her know when we would be arriving. Nora was dismayed at my appearance and was bent on fattening me up.

We gradually settled into the life of 11 Patterdale Gardens. I had to make arrangements for my confinement as Nora had heard that owing to the large number of women expecting babies places in hospitals and maternity homes were scarce. I went to Nora's doctor who rang round a number of nursing homes, but the best that could be done was to go into Wallsend Hospital for the actual confinement, stay two days then go home to be nursed by a visiting midwife or to have the actual confinement at Nora's. However I decided on the hospital.

Not surprisingly Martin was going through a very mummyish phase, yelling when put to bed and wanting to be played with all the time. He also missed Rex very much and had bouts of saying plaintively, "I want my Daddy" and forever playing at going on a ship to Lagos. That and building houses to bomb were his favourite games. He had learnt about bombing from the boys on the ship. He still had a very troublesome cold and cough and I sometimes had to take him into my bed when he kept waking in the night, because it was too cold to keep getting up. He had been a great favourite on the boat and was very spoilt, and I had the job of unspoiling him! It was impossible to imagine the heat of Lagos.

It was very cold in Newcastle at this time, all the pipes in the house frozen and snow thick and frozen on the ground. It was difficult to get acclimatised. Joyce Bailey sent some good warm clothes for Martin, which Andrew had grown out of. I have all the letters which passed between Rex and myself at this time, so I am not relying absolutely on memory. Martin told Nora that he had a nice Mummy and she said "You are a lucky boy." "Yes, I'm a very lucky boy,'cos I have a nice Daddy as well. He is in Lagos." Often at this time Martin picked up a pretend phone and said such things as "Hallo Daddy, I ve got my new braces on" or more often, "Hallo Daddy, I'm a naughty boy. At this time my brother Fred was a full lieutenant and in charge of a minesweeper.

I realised that Tom and Nora were very good to Martin and me at this time accepting us in their home and willing to put up with and entertain a small child whilst longing all the time for a child of their own. Tom often played with and read to Martin in the evenings or worked in the garden with him. Nora had been able to get a promise, however reluctantly given, of leave whilst I was in hospital in order to look after Martin. Tom had made a wooden cot frame and Nora used some Kano cloth I had to make the cradle part and it was very suitable for the purpose. During this period Tom's mother was ill and died, and there was a lot of coming and going between Tom's family and Nora and Tom.

Of course Martin's vocabulary was increasing all the time and he was saying such things as "Uncle is pulling my leg" and when shown the picture of an owl said, "Toowit toowoo, goodnight to you. He said it to me in Lagos. He was a kind old owl. I want to write to the kind old owl in Lagos." At one time he was very excited because George, Tom's brother, took him for rides on a tram and trolley buses.

There was a false alarm when Hilary was due to be born when I had gone to the cinema with Nora one evening. On our return home we decided I should go to the Wallsend Hospital where I stayed for two days having several doses of castor oil. As nothing happened I was sent home and went back a week later when there was no doubt that this was it. I was put to sleep for the actual birth and had six stitches, but everything was normal after that and for no reason I could account for Hilary was pronounced "a very special baby" by the nurses. As babies do not always arrive when predicted, there was room for me in the hospital for ten days rather than the promised two.

Children were not allowed as visitors and Nora had to find someone to look after Martin when she visited. At one time she had to take him to the office. On his birthday Nora took him to town and let him choose a present from herself and Tom - he chose a cloth teddy bear. Nora made him a birthday cake. When the day came to go home Nora brought Martin in a taxi and he was thrilled - beaming all over to see me and Hilary and some other babies. He talked to Sister. On the way home the baby was registered as Hilary Joan.

Don's letters to Rex during this period, without actually saying so, give the impression that she felt she was being a considerable imposition on Tom and Nora, an impression perhaps due to her listing all that that they did for her. On the other hand, Nora's diary tends to convey that she was carrying on much as usual, apart from the period immediately around Hilary's birth, though she was certainly put out by her two- to three-year old nephew's behaviour, which varied from the charming (mostly to strangers) to the dreadful. Tom's mother died suddenly and unexpectedly in January, and this of course occasioned a great upheaval. Don was not the only person being put up in these difficult months at the end of the war and she did help out with household tasks.

On 3rd June 1945, Nora came with Martin, Hilary and myself to London to stay with Mum and Dad. We had chosen that time as Fred was home on leave. Dad and Fred met us at Kings Cross. At 37 Ashley Road, Mum, Connie, Janet and David were waiting for us, seven years after I had left home. Auntie Beth arrived from the office. It was a great reunion. Mum and Dad had rearranged the whole house for our arrival. Nora was staying with Connie. I saw a lot of bomb damage.

Life at this time was not at all easy. Mum and Dad were getting old and Mum not at all well, and they were not used to small children. Martin missed his father and was very difficult to deal with. I was looking for other accommodation for Rex's arrival as living at home was not going to work. There was nothing to be had anywhere near London and then CMS came up with a suggestion that we might rent Mrs McKeenan's house at Broadstairs, which would be available except for a room for herself and her two small sons when they were on holiday from their boarding school. They had been missionaries and her husband had been drowned and she was hoping to get a residential job. Eventually it was fixed up that we would rent her house at £3.3.0 a week!

Joan Cox came to 37 Ashley Road for a night in July and we talked our heads off. She was staying at St Julian's and later on I went with Hilary by train to see her there, leaving Martin with Con. I had not seen Joan for seven years and she seemed just the same.

Don's move to London came after the end of the war. Later in life Don stated that she and Rex were pacifists, but they did not make an issue of it, and they did not object to my being a member of the Cadet Corps which was compulsory at the secondary school I attended, because they did not want me to stand out. However, it is not at all clear that they were pacifist in 1945. Rex's comments on the war news show a sense of identification with the advancing allied forces, and any worry about the suffering was overwhelmed by relief that the war was coming to an end. Don's letters did not remark on anything but the victory celebrations.

Once she was in London, Don went to see Dr Anderson at CMS, and he said that she should see a Medical Board the following week. "There was only Dr Anderson & two old boys on the Board & the Chairman did all the talking, just asked me a lot of trivial questions, at least they seemed so to me." She later received a letter from the (unnamed) Chairman saying that the Board had made a minute as follows: "Returned in fair health. To see a Specialist." In the absence of any other information she assumed that a gynaecologist was intended. When she sent Dr Anderson the bills for her confinement she said that she thought a specialist unnecessary. Otherwise Don's letters from this time do not add significantly to this account. Rex's letters help to give a picture of life in Lagos, which will be described later. The decision that Rex would return in August was taken very suddenly, and for months there had been a lot of doubt about when he would be coming. He must have returned by plane, the first time this would have happened.

Rex came home in the middle of the night in August 1945 and saw his baby daughter for the first time. Soon after Rex's arrival we had Hilary baptised. Bill Bailey, who was to be her godfather, came to perform the ceremony and Joan Cox, as godmother, came as well, so we had a little party at 37 Ashley Road. Evelyn Shepherd was her second godmother. We then moved to the house in Broadstairs where we spent six months. This was a peaceful and happy time, when we found all the walks around Broadstairs. Martin was a good walker, trotting along beside the pram quite happily. It was not easy to go very far afield with two small children, but we had quite long walks.

When it was time for us to return to Lagos, there was no ship's passage for myself and the children as the authorities were getting all the men back to their jobs before the women and children who had to wait. We returned to 37 Ashley Road, said au revoir to Rex in April 1946, and were set to stay there until we were offered passages, when a call came from Nora and Tom. Nora had given birth to her first daughter and wanted my help at home. Rex's father and stepmother agreed to have Martin to stay and I went to Newcastle with Hilary who was then twelve months old. I had been there a week or two when we were offered passages to Lagos, so I had to return to Thornton Heath, get Rex's Dad to bring Martin, pack up and get us to Tilbury. I cannot remember anything about the journey to Tilbury, only about the queues with passports etc, lugging a heavy thirteen month old and trying to control a lively four year old. We eventually boarded the ship which was crowded with women and children joining the male member of the family in Nigeria. We shared a cabin with a Methodist missionary's wife with a girl and boy the same ages as mine. There was nowhere for Hilary to sleep so she had to spend nights as well as days in the pram. The food was very unsuitable for small children and during the voyage Hilary's practically sole diet was biscuits and milk. There were a number of single missionaries on board, mostly CMS, and eight of them shared a cabin. The voyage was a nightmare for me with the cramped conditions, poor food and restlessness of the children. Hilary suffered from prickly heat through sleeping in a confined space, but was perfect. Martin has never been allowed to forget his words on popping up from under the table in the dining room, having refused to eat mashed potatoes mixed with pickle - "I'm hungry, I am." When we arrived at Lagos Rex came on board to meet us. Among my first words were, "I want to sleep for a fortnight!"

One incident on this voyage made a great impression upon me. One day I was sitting on deck with the other CMS people, with Hilary in the pram, when I realised that Martin was not with us. Leaving the others in charge of Hilary I rushed round the ship looking for him, in a state of panic. Eventually I caught sight of him lying on his tummy under a lifeboat, looking at the water below. There was nothing to prevent a fall. I grabbed him by the legs to safety.

We settled into the CMS house in Broad Street, the main road. Martin joined the kindergarten class at the CMS Girls' School, the only white child in a class of about twenty. It is interesting that at this stage of his development he did not distinguish between black and white people. He the whole class of Africans and three white children at his fifth birthday party. When asked if his teacher was an English or an African woman, he thought for a time and then said, "I don't know."

During this tour Martin had whooping cough and measles at the same time and was really very ill. Rex and I took turns to sleep on a camp bed in his room as the cough was so distressing he was needing attention sometimes every quarter of an hour. The doctor came to see him every day. When he was getting better I had to take him to the Creek Hospital to have the scabs caused by the measles removed. This caused him to scream so that all the nurses in the hospital came running to see what all the noise was about. Hilary caught the infections but very lightly.

In September 1947, having had a trouble-free pregnancy, I gave birth to a baby girl in the Creek Hospital. For this time I was in hospital Martin stayed with Harry and Nellie Jobling at Abeokuta, and Dorothy and Fred Davies stayed in our Broad Street house to supervise Regina, the girl who looked after Hilary, then two years five months old. When it was time to baptise the baby, we chose Margaret Potts and Dorothy Davies as godmothers and ffolliott Powell as godfather. The baby was baptised Margaret Ruth Ayodele by Canon Howells in

Lagos Cathedral. (The Yoruba name Ayodele means "Joy comes to the house.") When Martin realised that Margaret had a Yoruba second name he called himself Martin Babatunde ("Father comes again").

On April 30th 1948 we flew home for leave, staying for a few days at the CMS Missionary Home in Streatham. From here we visited my parents in Thornton Heath. We then moved up to Neston, near Birkenhead, where we rented a house found for us by my former vicar, Clifford Martin, now the Bishop of Liverpool.

Martin attended the school next door and became great friends with his teacher, Mrs Coventry, who sometimes came to tea. We explored the countryside around Neston and once Martin and I did a six mile walk.

This was rather a sad time for us as we were preparing Martin and his clothes to stay at home when we returned to Lagos. He was to be a boarder at the CMS St Michael's School at Limpsfield, near Oxted, Surrey. The job of taking Martin to London to meet the school party travelling to the school was one of the saddest I have ever undertaken. He was only six and a half and I shall never forget my feelings as I said good-bye to him at Victoria as he was given into the hands of the mistress travelling with the children, and I turned away in tears. It made a lasting impression on me.

St Michael's was a boarding school set up by CMS for the children of its missionaries, and Gordon Hewitt, the CMS historian, says of it: "Old Michaelians when questioned about their memories of the school tend to be puzzled when asked about the psychological effects of the long separation from their parents. Nearly all of those who were at St Michael's during this period [to 1942] seem to have been happy there." I do not think that this was my experience in the lower school at a slightly later period. During the holidays I stayed with aunt Con, and when compiling this account I wrote to Con's daughter, my cousin Janet, living in New Zealand, to ask what she could remember of the impression that our family made, coming and going at odd intervals, and depending on their relatives for help. She replied "My brother and I have very little memory of this time you spent with us while your parents were in Africa, we both remembered that you were very quiet when you came home from Boarding School."

Now, Don's letters and family anecdotes show clearly that at the age of three, I was a confident and outgoing boy, making myself at home in the household of the Dixons, who at that time had no children of their own, and quite happy to start talking to strangers. At the age of seven I was quiet and withdrawn. It seems very likely that it was the experience of boarding school that brought about this complete reversal. Of the school itself I can remember little apart from interminable services in the chapel, and revolting food that we were obliged to choke down. I may have gone sleepwalking on one occasion. There were kind friends of my parents who used to take me out on hillsides covered with bracken, and bracken has ever since had good associations for me.

During this leave we were able to meet a number of people we knew including Miss Grimwood (Grimmie), retired Principal of the CMS Lagos Girls Schools, and the Clifford Martins who took us to a beach and had us to tea at their home in Liverpool. I also met Margaret Johnson, a doctor with whom I trained at Kennaway Hall and who had married and worked in India. She was speaking at a missionary meeting in Neston. I was very much struck by the fact that her very good looks had been spoilt by her life in

73

India. She had two children and was expecting another.

In November 1948 soon after Martin's departure we returned to Nigeria by ship and had a pleasant voyage. The house in Broad Street was again our home with our boy, John, to help me with the chores. It was Hilary's turn to attend the kindergarten class at the Girls School. The Wilkinsons, Elizabeth and Wilkie with their young daughter Gwynneth were living next door so Hilary and Gwynneth attended school together. An incident involving the cutting of Hilary's hair by Gwynneth is always remembered.

This was Rex's first tour as Manager of the Bookshop. In connection with his appointment, but rather belatedly, the African Staff Union presented him with an elaborately illuminated address, which reads as follows (with the correction of some spelling mistakes):

an address presented to

MR A. E. WYATT

ON THE OCCASION OF HIS PROMOTION AS THE

MANAGER C.M.S. BOOKSHOP, LAGOS

BY THE C.M.S. BOOKSHOP AFRICAN STAFF UNION

LAGOS DIOCESE

ON SATURDAY 11TH JUNE 1949

Dear Sir,

We, the undersigned representing the C.M.S. Bookshop African Staff Union, Lagos Diocese present you this address to mark the occasion of your being promoted Manager of the Bookshop, Lagos Diocese.

Arriving in the country on the 5th March 1936 you met nine Europeans on the staff, the last of whom you now succeed as the Manager, others having left for one reason or another.

During the shortage of European Staff caused by World War II, you as the only lieutenant of the substantive holder of the post, stood by him like ten strong men judging by the co-operation and support. We are not exaggerating if we say that with your co-operation the Union has succeeded in achieving some of its requests viz:-

(i) During the time you relieved the Manager in 1944, the Union desired the implementation of Tudor Davies report as was done in nearly all Departments of labour in the country. We highly appreciated the way and manner with which you tackled this problem ere the arrival of the manager as a result of which the Union was granted this request.

(ii) You took no less active part during the Harraging Report for compiling the figures which was highly commended by the manager Mr. W. D. Thompson.

When the news reached us that on your arrival from furlough you will assume the post of Manager as from 1st December 1948, this accorded us as a body a great pleasure. We hope you will make the fullest use of this opportunity to develop upon the foundations and schemes laid by your predecessor to endear you as well as him in the hearts of the public and the workers under you for the good that men do live for ever after them.

Your first step in the development scheme under your managership is being marked with promotion of five senior men as district and shop supervisors in April 1949. As you have begun well we do trust and hope that you will allow justice, patience tact and sympathy which are inseparable keys to success of any head of department be your guide. All our needs, requests and sufferings have been made known to the management including your good self.

We assure you, Sir, as a body, of our continuous co-operation and mutual understanding as already prevailing between us as employer and employees. We shall always remember you and family in our devotional prayers that God may guide you always in the discharge of the onerous duties entrusted to your care.

We are,
   Sir,
   Yours in His vineyard.
(Twelve signatures)

At the point where Rex took it over, the Bookshop had been developed into a large and successful commercial undertaking. It was the bookshop for the whole of the Lagos diocese and had a good many up-country branches. The senior staff would tour round these from time to time, keeping in touch, and supporting and checking on the clerks who ran them. Expansion in the north was a constant theme, and part of the work on tour was to set up new branches. On the negative side, there had evidently been constant staffing problems. The main way in which these were tackled comes out both in the address already quoted and in the one presented to him on his departure, which reads in part:

"WE record with pleasure that since your arrival in Nigeria in 1936, you have endeared yourself to the aspirations of the Staff in general, and when you were made Manager of this establishment in 1949, your first act was to promote five African members of the Staff to the post of District and Shop Supervisors. It was also through your generosity and tenacity of purpose that two members of the Staff retired on pension and gratuity in January, 1950.

TO foster the spirit of co-operation, you founded the Branch Conference as a means of bringing branch members together to exchange views for the general progress of the work. This has created great enthusiasm in members and has enhanced the cordial relationship between the Management and the Staff on the one hand and the African and European members of the Staff on the other. The carrying out of your project for establishing more new branches of the C.M.S. (Nigeria) Bookshops and of awarding scholarships to deserving African members of the Staff to enable them to study in the United Kingdom and qualify for more responsible posts in the establishment, will be a fitting crown for the efforts of an energetic Manager whose place it will be difficult to fill, but whose records of good work will remain indelible in our minds and in the archives of the C.M.S. (Nigeria) Bookshops."

I do not know whether these reforms were due to the Manager's initiative or to the Lagos Bookshop Committee, or to the wider discussions which were taking place around the whole enterprise. These discussions had undoubtedly included the chronic staffing problems, with the West African Bookshops failing to attract and keep good European staff, and at some stage it became clear that the only solution to the staffing problem was in training and making use of African staff. Wherever this view originated, it was the Manager who was responsible for implementing it.

Rex's letters home during his last tour show that he had much worry over a male member of staff whose wife was at home in Britain and who was in an intense relationship with one of the female staff members. She appears to have gone in for eyelash fluttering, because on one occasion another missionary was imitating her. Rex did his best to keep them apart, forbidding them to put their desks next to each other and on one occasion summoning the man up-country to oversee the adaptation of a building for a new branch and to change the clerk in another branch. The Bishop was asked to speak to the woman, but only did so in terms that were far too general. Eventually both resigned within a few days of each other, and on returning home the man asked his wife for a divorce. Rex wrote that this put CMS in a flap over protecting their good name. "I had never imagined that the relationship with Miss B had gone to such lengths."

The bookshop continued to be financially successful. On one occasion he wrote with some complacency that a request for money arrived from London after he had already sent them more than they were asking for.

> The following summer, 1949, Martin flew to Lagos for the summer holidays. He had not been very happy at school at times. My sister Connie, had looked after him in the shorter holidays but he was delighted to come to Lagos and he and Hilary were very pleased with one another's company. When it was time for Martin to return home we were able to find a young woman who was travelling on the same plane with her baby and who was willing to keep an eye on Martin. Connie was going to meet him in England and cable us when he arrived. The cable did not come when it

should have done and we were very worried so I rang up Lagos airport. The answer I got was that I would have heard if the plane had not arrived safely. About two days later there was a cable from Con saying the plane had broken down and was delayed at Tripoli. They were there for a day or two and the young mother was able to take the children to a beach where she put a baby's nappy on Martin so that he could bathe. We were thankful to hear from Con when the plane eventually arrived safely.

During this tour we gradually came to the conclusion that this must be our last one as a family in Lagos, for the sake of the children's health and schooling. We flew home in April 1950, knowing that at least the children and I would be staying at home. CMS had found us a cottage belonging to the lady of the manor to rent at a very low rent in the village of Hawkley, Surrey. It had a lovely vegetable garden and a gardener came once or twice a week to work in it, so we never went without vegetables. Sometimes the lady of the manor sent us a chicken to cook. Hilary attended the village school where she was very happy. During the time at Hawkley Joan Cox came to stay with me and Hilary and Margaret whilst Rex was away on Bookshop business. Whilst at Hawkley I heard of the death of Florence Allshorn, but as Rex was away on Bookshop business I was unable to go to the funeral.

Rex and I took it in turns to look at suitable houses for sale somewhere in the South where we might settle. In the meantime CMS had suggested that Rex might return to Lagos as Manager of the CMS Bookshop for nine months and come home for three months when he could visit publishers etc. We agreed to this plan. We found a house to suit us at Temple Ewell, three miles from Dover at a price of £2,700, which considering it had two reception rooms, breakfast room, kitchen, study, four bedrooms, boxroom and a bathroom was very cheap. Houses in the Dover area were among the cheapest in the country as during the war Dover had suffered badly from shelling and had not yet been rebuilt, so was not considered a desirable area.

When Rex's leave ended he flew back to Lagos leaving me at Valetta, our Temple Ewell house, with the children. Martin had left St Michael's Limpsfield and with Hilary was attending daily St Michael's School, a private school in the village run by Miss Kennett. We had made enquiries about schools and been told the local council school did not have a good reputation.

This was a very difficult time for me. Martin particularly was very badly behaved and sometimes I was at my wits' end. He did very well at school. We attended Church, which was very sleepy and uninspiring, and I joined the Mothers' Union. There was nothing to do in the village and there were no women of my own age anywhere near. Money was scarce, so I had to be careful over housekeeping. It was difficult to keep the house warm as the central heating fed by an old boiler at the back of a smokeless coal fire was inadequate for the radiators. At one time I got very depressed, which must have been communicated to Rex who asked CMS to send someone to find out how I was faring, and someone came down from CMS to visit us.

Because of these difficulties, Rex told CMS that his time in Lagos would be coming to an end. CMS were not at all happy with this decision. Micky Davidson wrote Rex a "hurtful letter", and the visit he made to Don in Temple Ewell, mentioned above, may have been to do with the fact that Rex had cited her difficulties as the reason for not continuing. For a while Rex felt that he was attacked from opposite sides by Micky and Don. But he stuck to his decision and the last weeks of his tour were spent in inducting his successor. Despite the unsatisfactory way in which it ended–Bookshop staff wanted to know why he was leaving so soon after being made manager–the time in Lagos had been fairly happy and definitely useful to the missionary effort.

The letters written by Rex in 1944/45 and 1950/51 give some idea of the life there.

In Lagos the Wyatt family had been part of a missionary community which seems to have included the Mission Secretary, teachers, other people involved in education, medical workers, and people passing through on their way "home" or "up-country", as well as other bookshop staff. There was an expectation that Lagos missionaries would provide hospitality for those passing through or staying there temporarily. The Bookshop Manager was paid an allowance for hospitality. The hospitality would be reciprocated when Rex travelled up-country himself. These visits were very much welcomed by the isolated workers, who were sometimes without other European company and working all hours.

The following extended excerpt from one of Rex's letters in 1945 is not particularly typical. There is little that is typical–the previous day's instalment had two doctors mending Rex's typewriter. The excerpt is intended to give a flavour of the travelling and provide another glimpse of missionary life away from Lagos.

[Dated 15 June 1945, relating to 14 June]

I finished at Ilesha Bookshop during the morning and after a late lunch set out to Ado Ekiti. The road was very bad, in parts it was dangerous, and to cap it

81

all while we were running through the hills we ran into very heavy rain. We had one or two unpleasant skids [He had an African driver, whom he has described as a good driver] and my nerves were decidedly ragged by the time we arrived at Ado Ekiti. It was twenty to five when we arrived at the hospital and I had to wait two hours before I could see Dr. Eva [Weddigen] as she was coping with over two hundred women with their babies. Just as it was getting dusk I set out for Dolly's house on the top of the hill; when we arrived there were no keys, no wood and no water. I had arranged to come back to the hospital for dinner and I suggested to Dr. Eva that it would be better if I moved to one of the rest houses and she promised to send a note up to the D.O. [District Officer] in the morning. It was approaching eleven o'clock when I got to the top of the hill again and I went straight to bed, completely fagged out. This morning we loaded everything into the car again and said good-bye to Dolly's house. The approach to the house is a most difficult one and running up down would take petrol and time. For the first part it is steadily up hill, then at a very steep part there is a sharp left-hand turn followed by a right-hand one flanked by a sheer drop on one side and the face of the hill on the other – not at all pleasant in the dark. I have had all of my meals at the hospital today but alone as my timetable has not fitted in with Dr. Eva's. Tonight she has gone up to chop with the D.O. as some mutual friends passing through are staying with him for the night. I am now installed in the upper rest-house which is only ten minutes walk from the hospital. There is a magnificent view and it is quiet there. It is time for me to return to my rest house as I am feeling very sleepy. Dr. Eva hasn't returned yet but I shall see her at breakfast in the morning before she goes off on trek for the day.

Saturday 16/6/45

As I finished my stock-taking yesterday I have been able to enjoy a lazy day today. During the past week I have completed four stock-takings and covered over three hundred miles so I haven't done badly. Tommy (W.D. Thompson, the Manager) thought I wouldn't keep to my programme but the hardest week is over and I am working to schedule. To return to yesterday: to my surprise and delight there were some letters waiting for me at the Bookshop, including one from you......

On my travels I have been trying to collect information about reading rooms and this morning I saw the D.O. here and got his views on them. Dr. Eva returned from trek this afternoon just before four o'clock and while we were having tea Bishop Phillips arrived; he is on tour at present and Eva has invited him to dinner, he is spending the night in Dolly's house and travels on again after the morning service tomorrow......

Last night we had heavy rain and today it has been delightfully cool, almost chilly in fact. Dr. Eva seems to be working all the time, she seems to have practically no time to rest but she is very insistent that I should rest as much as possible. She told me this afternoon that I looked very tired when I arrived, I think it was probably the result of the journey from Ilesha. I am feeling much rested today and am looking forward to a quiet Sunday tomorrow......

Sunday 17/6/45

Bishop Phillips did not come down to dinner last night after all; he sent a message down that he would come to breakfast instead, after service – but it is now half past eleven and he hasn't appeared yet. When I came down at half past eight this morning I was surprised to find Mr. Hughes of the Y.M.C.A. here. He is on his way to Benin and Port Harcourt but just as it was getting dark yesterday he had a puncture and owing to a lack of tools he couldn't get it mended until three o'clock this morning so he came up here for breakfast and a rest. He is enjoying a sleep now and he is going on after lunch.

Evening. This afternoon Eva and I went for a walk. On our way we met the D.O. and his wife, we strolled along together and then went up to his house for a cup of tea. I was presented with some nice lettuces from the prison garden to take on to Ikare with me tomorrow. I had a very holy bath this evening, my bathroom is adjacent to another which was being used at the time for a Bible study group. There is no door in between but only a large cupboard across the doorway; as a result they heard me splashing and I heard them. I washed my legs and feet to a hymn, my arms to prayers and my body to Bible reading. Such a holy bath I never had before.

Tomorrow morning I go on to Ikare.

The relationship with the community around the family in Lagos was partly social, partly religious and partly work-based.

Social life included regular tennis in the early evening, the number of participants varying according to commitments, giving meals and going to meals given to other people. These were frequently accompanied by the playing of gramophone records and by games, the names of which mean nothing to me.

There would often be a prayer meeting during the week, with people taking it in turns to provide the hospitality and to lead. Writing from Newcastle in January 1945, Don commented:

"This is P[rayer] M[eeting] evening & I am wondering where you have had it this week. I think you must be very good at leading P.M.s as you always manage to induce people to be vocal. Perhaps that is not well put, but you know what I mean."

On Sundays when Don was absent, Rex would frequently attend two services, or perhaps more, at the Cathedral, the Colonial Church, or elsewhere. Although he was a Lay Reader, he did not often take services or preach for an adult congregation, but in 1944/45 he had some responsibility (it is not quite clear what) for a Children's Service, which had attendances of well over a hundred. During his last tour he mentioned preaching two sermons, one of which, unusually, was written, and not good.

Don in her first batch of letters made some comments about mission, but Rex in his says little about the missionary effort in general. In once of his tours up country he remarked that American missionaries did not take advantage of the experience of those who had been in the country longer, but he does not say in what way. There is a similar problem about the sense of vocation. It is evident that Rex and Don had an intense devotional life, to which there are occasional oblique or half-apologetic references—Rex told Don *after* the event that he has gone without breakfast on Sundays during Lent, knowing she would disapprove.

In 1945 he wrote to her saying:

"In praying for me please remember these weaknesses of mine (1) Short temper (2) Lack of loyalty in speaking of Tommy (3) Too much interest in myself and my own soul." More regular are the accounts of what each has been reading. But of what has been driving them there is little mention. In 1945 Rex wrote: "At times I feel very downcast because I am not with you but I know I have much to be thankful for in having a good wife and two healthy children. A vocation such as ours must involve sacrifice otherwise it would not be a true calling by God. We must pray that God will use these hard things to His own honour and glory and to the upbuilding of His kingdom on earth." About three months later he was saying "I am afraid that a missionary vocation and a settled home life seldom go hand in hand and at heart I am still firmly convinced of my vocation; I know that I am not a good missionary in many ways but that doesn't stop me being one altogether."

In reply to this Don wrote:

"I would like to give you a gentle reminder that a missionary vocation is not determined by place, and I ~~think~~ know that there must be many who are following a missionary vocation while living at home – indeed it would be a very sad state of affairs if there weren't." On his last tour in 1950, however, Rex was still saying that "I still believe that God wants me here at the present time in spite of all our difficulties."

In Rex's case the vocation took a very specific form. But he was not only involved in Bookshop work, he also helped others, such as the Girls School, with their work, specifically their accounts. This help extended outside the immediate CMS ambit to the Scouts. During the last tour he also acted as Mission Secretary for two brief periods.

The Bookshop work included occasional items which were not part of the regular routine. For instance, there does not seem to have been a system for increasing wages in line with inflation. In 1945 Rex was taking home a lot of work on COLA, the cost of living award, and it appears that recipients attributed their increases in wages to the work he had put in. He was also expected to do a certain amount of bookshop business, such as dealing with publishers, when he was on leave.

Living in Lagos was an urban way of life. The Olympic Hotel was either next to the house in Broad Street or very close to it, and Rex would be disturbed by the piano playing far into the night. Nevertheless, the conditions were very different from those in England. The climate was always very hot and humid, and at certain seasons oppressively so. This imposed a particular rhythm on the day, with a rest in the early afternoon being common. The temperature was a regular topic in the letters home. Tropical diseases always threatened. Worries about children's health have already been mentioned. Quite young white people are mentioned as dying after a short illness. For a period in 1951, Rex was not at his best, and "low fever" was diagnosed. The household kept two servants, a male cook and a "small boy". For some time in 1950, Rex was employing these without actually having fixed their wages, the small boy being aged 26. This contrasted with the situation is South Africa where there had been a succession of unsatisfactory adolescent girls, and Winifred Noordendorp and Don began to think they would do better without one.

There were always money worries in the background. Both had to be extremely careful. Rex always kept a detailed account of expenditure, and could tell where every penny had gone, and it seems that Don may have done the same, at least at certain periods. They were used to a regime of make do and mend. Don would make many of her own clothes, sheets, curtains, loose covers and so on, knit socks for Rex, and mend clothes as necessary. Rex owned a cobbler's last, though I am not sure that he ever used it. He would darn his socks, and get collars turned so as to make shirts last longer. These were fairly common practices at the time, but they show that having servants was not an indicator of prosperity. My parents would never put bone-handled knives in hot water, and when I mentioned to them that another missionary family had said that a bone-handled knife that came apart in hot water was not worth having, my father said it was all right for them – they had money. One of the issues to do with leaving Nigeria was whether Rex would be able to get a job at the sort of level he had attained. When Micky Davidson from CMS went to see Don in Temple Ewell, Rex wrote to her:

> "I am sorry you mentioned the financial side to Micky, I have kept off it through pride; I am not good at begging for myself and they should have enough facts to realise our position with money." I do not know how they paid for the private school in Temple Ewell.

There were compensations. On his final tour of the country, when staff knew that Rex was leaving, they gave him a number of presents as he went round. Most of these were pieces of cloth, and Don still had them fifty years later.

However, after nine months Rex came home and we made the decision that he should stay at home. This way of life did not suit any of us. Rex was hoping to find a job in Canterbury so that we could stay in Valetta, but there was nothing for him there. CMS then suggested that we might go to Uganda where the Manager of the Uganda Bookshop, Kampala, was soon to retire, and Rex could take his place. [CMS was not responsible for the Uganda Bookshop, which was run directly by the Church in Uganda, but had its own reasons for wanting to help out.] There was a school in Kampala which the children could attend up to the age of twelve, and as there was no secondary education in Kampala for expatriates, they could attend boarding schools in Kenya. We felt this was a very big step to take and needed a lot of thought. Margaret Potts who was then the leader of the Community at St Julians suggested that we should have time to think about it in a stay of six weeks at St Julians, with the children staying at Farleys, the children's house across the fields. We accepted this suggestion.

Probably taken on Rex's farewell tour at Ibadan. The cloth shown on the cover was also presented to him at this time.

Part 6.

Uganda

In Uganda Don and Rex lived continuously together, so there is no correspondence, and the only additional detail comes from my own memories. The section of Don's memoir dealing with Uganda is less of a connected narrative and more a collection of episodes in logical sequences.

At St Julians, Rex and I had a lovely large room overlooking the lake. In the mornings Rex worked in the garden and I in the bedrooms most of the time, though I did have a short period in the kitchen. In the afternoons we had a study group with Dorothy Alton as leader, the other members being Marjorie Norton on leave from India, Janet Clarke from Nigeria and Diana Minchall. There was sometimes a little evening duty and then we were free. We had plenty of time to think and read. We saw the children quite frequently. They had been given lessons by Rex which they had to work at, and were taken on outings by the members of the Community staffing the Children's House.

By the end of our time at St Julians, Rex and I had arrived quite independently at the decision that we should go to Uganda. After letting Valetta and making our preparations we set sail for East Africa. It was March 1952.

The big zinc-lined chests were packed up again and sent off to travel in the hold. The house was let furnished, and items that we were leaving behind, but not for the use of the tenants were put into the small ground floor study, with a padlock on the door. The ship went through the Suez canal, and my main memory of the voyage is of the armed police in Port Said.

The outstanding event on the voyage was the children's Fancy Dress Parade. I managed to find enough material in our luggage to make a long floral dress with white apron and mob cap and a big black spider for Hilary to go as Little Miss Muffet. The ship's kitchen provided the bowl and wooden spoon. Martin wore khaki shirt and shorts, a wide cummerbund and khaki puttees, and I made a policeman's navy blue helmet from an old felt hat for him to go as an African policeman. Hilary won first prize. Margaret was too small to go to this event as she was in bed with a chest cold. The ship's doctor had prescribed for her, and Rex and I took it in turns to stay with her. She had her share of the goodies handed out to the children.

On arrival in Mombasa we boarded a train to Kampala, a 600/700 miles journey taking two days and a night. At all the stations we felt were in India rather than Africa as there were so many Indians. The Indians brought to Kenya to build the railway had stayed and multiplied and there were now a great number in Kenya and Uganda and in fact all over Africa, as they were very evident in South Africa when we were there. They were great traders and ran nearly all the dukas (shops).

The train journey between Nairobi and Kampala was one I was to make six times a year from 1955 to 1960, going to

91

and from boarding school. The journey took 26 hours, the trains averaging 20 miles an hour because of the steep gradients. The climb up and down the east side of the Rift Valley was spectacular, as the track angled across the face of the escarpment, giving views of the floor of the valley with its lakes and volcanoes.

We arrived in Kampala on a Sunday and were taken to the CMS Guest House on Namirembe until our house was ready. We were all hot and dirty and longing for a bath but there was no hot water, the boys who built the fire to heat bath water all being off duty on Sundays. (it is amazing the bits one remembers.)

We soon settled into the house provided for us and were able to employ Yessero, a "boy" usually employed by the Reggie Hopkins family who were on leave. When they returned to Namirembe Yessero refused to go back to them, so Yessero was our "boy" until the end of our time in Uganda (12 years). He did not live in but in a small house on the hill (Namirembe) with his wife and family.

Soon after our arrival we had a visit from Joan Cox who was headmistress of Gayaza High School 14 miles from Kampala. We had not met for some years since the time she visited us at Hawkley.

Namirembe is a hill rising above Kampala Town with the Cathedral at the top. The first cathedral had been built about 1889 and was preached in by Bishop Tucker in 1890 to a thousand people. In 1892 this was replaced by a remarkable structure built by the Baganda, the roof of which was supported by the trunks of 500 forest trees, in which on Christmas Day he preached to 5000 people. The cathedral as we knew it was built some years later,

> The missionaries' houses, including those of
> the doctors and nurses of Mengo Hospital, which
> is built on the slopes of the hill, were situated
> around the slopes of the hill below the cathedral.
> From Namirembe there is a view of Kampala and
> the hills around.

Although Namirembe was counted as one of the seven hills of Kampala (it seems that every city built on hills has seven of them) it was definitely not an urban setting. The missionaries' bungalows were scattered around, with considerable distances between them, except on the side away from town where the buildings of Mengo hospital clustered together. A grassy slope stretched down from the cathedral, to which the road from town (surfaced for the Queen's visit) spiralled upward. There were two or three buildings for diocesan offices, and tennis courts, tennis again being a staple of social life. As Kampala was 4,000 feet above sea level, the climate was comfortably warm rather than oppressive. There were minor hazards, such as jiggers burrowing under toenails, but major ones, such as poisonous snakes, were very rare. For European families it was a friendly environment and greatly preferable to Lagos. The children roamed freely about the hill. On one occasion the boys climbed up onto the cathedral roof and scratched our initials on the dome. We then heard that the archdeacon was going to inspect the roof, so we climbed up again and painted them over. The two types of black paint did not match, but we never heard anything about it. We would go into town, walking or getting lifts one way or both.

The missionary community on Namirembe was fairly self-contained. There was some interaction with the university staff on Makerere, an adjoining hill. The main European settlement, of officials and business people, was on Kololo on the other side of town. That community had its own church in town, and we might attend the morning service there and the evening service in the cathedral chapel. The children had little interaction with the Baganda population, local commerce being dominated by the Asian settlers who mostly originated from Gujarat.

The bookshop where Rex worked was in the middle of Kampala, and although it was essentially a church enterprise, it had a good range of books on all subjects. There were branches around the country, and Rex would visit these from time to time.

> The European School was in Kampala 2½ miles away. The wives of the missionaries on a rota drove the children to and from school, and as it was not always easy for Rex to take our turn, we decided that I should learn to drive. I was taught by an Indian woman complete in sari and after a second go at the test was declared competent to drive.
>
> The children did very well at school. Martin was eight when he started there. One day he surprised the Chaplain who taught scripture there, when he asked at assembly, "What is the period before the flood called?", not expecting an answer. However, Martin put up his hand and answered "antediluvian".
>
> We discovered when Margaret brought her teacher home to tea and the teacher asked how much longer Margaret would be going to the dentist on Wednesday afternoons, that she had been playing truant because she hated a certain lesson. She had been waiting in the little park beside the school until the car came to pick up the children, which was a dangerous thing to do in Kampala.
>
> One of Martin's escapades which I discovered was that Peter Hopkins who was living with us on school days and Martin sometimes at night climbed out of

their bedroom window and wandered round Namirembe hill.

We had two black labrador dogs whilst in our first Namirembe house. That particular breed did not do very well and both died, one a painful death through being poisoned. Then we had Sally, a Scottish terrier. She mated with a standard spaniel. The result was three puppies born on Easter Day while we were at church. We always said there were three important events on that Sunday beside the puppies. It was Martin's tenth birthday, the Queen's birthday and Easter Day! We decided to keep Mickey, the most lovable of the puppies, and suitable homes were found for the other two. He was the funniest looking dog.

One day Mr Patterson, father of Mollie who taught at Gayaza, a retired civil servant who looked after the grounds of the Cathedral, saw a boy in Mengo Village leading an owl by a rope. He took the owl from him and brought it to Martin to look after. It was injured and could not fly, so Martin kept it in a store room under the house with the door open and fed it on hard boiled egg and water. One morning it must have been well enough to fly and it disappeared. The strange thing was that at our next house, "Golden Gates", we found a baby owl under a tree having fallen from the next. We treated it in exactly the same way as the first one and eventually it flew away one night.

On Namirembe we saw many visitors as people passing through Kampala often stayed with friends including us, or at the Guest House. Among them was Beryl Pring, with whom I travelled on my first voyage to Nigeria, now married and with two adopted children, Martin and Hilary. Dorothy Alton and Marjorie Norton were also among them. Faith Sharland had one of her babies at Mengo Hospital. Then there were Hilda

Stovold and Elizabeth and Peter Bostock from Nairobi. Peter, who was Provost of Nairobi Cathedral, and Elizabeth were very good to Martin when he was at the Duke of York School, Nairobi, as they had him out on the short holidays when we could not get to Nairobi.

Our first holiday in Uganda was spent at Lake Nabugabo where there were rather primitive huts to rent and very hard beds. We had a Ford Popular car which with the five of us and Yessero, who was going to cook for us, and of course our baggage, was packed to overflowing. Most of the luggage including provisions had to go on the roof rack. We were not very far out of Kampala when the roof rack started slipping and we had to get out and secure it. We arrived eventually and settled into one of the family houses. There was nothing to do apart from bathing, going out in an old boat, reading and going for short walks, but it was a restful and enjoyable holiday. Mr and Mrs Robinson, mother and father of one of the Mengo nurses lived there and we were invited to tea with them.

Another holiday was spent on Sharp's Island near Kabale in Kigezi country. This was a small island owned by Dr and Mrs Sharp, who allowed families to use a holiday house there. From there we were able to visit the Leper Island where Dr Parry, Margaret's father, was in charge, and to take part in a Sunday service with a congregation of leper patients and staff. We were taken to and from the island in a large rowing boat manned by Africans. This visit was an amazing experience.

On the way back from Sharp's Island we noticed that we had a trail of liquid behind us. On examination we discovered a stone had penetrated the petrol tank. Martin had some plasticine with him so Rex made a plug of that which lasted to our next destination fifty miles away, where we were staying the night with friends. The next day we were able to get the hole repaired and return to Kampala.

Yet another holiday was spent at Turi, Kenya, which was a boarding school for European children. On the way the fan belt of the car broke, so Rex thumbed a lift to the nearest town for a new one whilst we all waited by the roadside for quite a long time. However, Rex fixed the new belt and we went on our way, arriving much later in the dark than expected. It was holiday time for the school and the only residents very kindly gave us supper and led us to the Sanatorium which was to be our holiday home. After the weekend Rex returned to Kampala and Gwen Cashmore came from Gayaza to spend the holiday with us. We were able to use the swimming pool and to pick any of the many vegetables from the school garden. I had my 50th birthday there duly celebrated. Rex came to collect us when it was time to go home.

Our last holiday in Uganda was spent at a beach near Mombasa in a rented holiday cottage on the shore. I do not think Martin was with us. There we nearly lived in the sea and on the clean sandy beach in glorious sunshine. Here I was very nervous at times because Margaret, who was at a difficult stage, would go off by herself for miles along the beach, which it was not safe to do.

We flew home for leave in 1955/56 in three hops, making the first stop at Juba, where Jean Drinkwater joined us. At our stop in Malta we stayed overnight at the Valetta Hotel. The children were given their evening meal in their bedrooms. When Jean, Rex and I went down to dinner we discovered that men were not allowed in the dining room without jackets. As Rex had left his on the plane because of the heat he borrowed Martin's maroon school blazer, very short in the sleeves for him. As a consequence the three of us had a hilarious meal, much better than going without.

It was a very cold winter. The night before flying back to Uganda, which we were doing in three hops again, we stayed with Alice and Stan, Rex's sister and brother-in-law in Southall. The train in which we travelled to London from Temple Ewell was unheated and we arrived there really frozen. However, Alice had a roaring coal fire which soon thawed us.

Our flight was very late setting off as there was engine trouble. We had two trips out to the plane and back again to the airport before we finally set off. It seemed a very flimsy plane and there was a draught from the badly fitting door. We eventually landed at Nice, which was not our destination for the first leg, and were put into a hotel. There bedrooms were Victorian style with valences round the beds and red and white furnishings, much to the amusement of the children.

The next day we flew on but had to land at an air force base (El Addam) in the desert because of engine trouble. Here it was raining, quite an event in this part of the world where it only rained about .once a year. Due to the lack of adequate guest accommodation the passengers on our flight had to split families. In our case Martin shared a room with Rex and me; Hilary shared with two maiden ladies and Margaret with a young mother with two small children. In the morning we were given breakfast and then embarked for the next leg of our journey, which was to Khartoum. Here it was very hot indeed. The children were given an early evening meal and were amused when the waiter asked them what they would like to drink, suggesting whiskey. The next leg of the journey was uneventful and we arrived safely at Entebbe.

The planes we flew in for this leave were Vickers Vikings, which were, I think, unpressurised. They certainly flew lower than modern planes. They must have had some form of heating, but nothing to cool them down when they had been standing in the sun for a couple of hours in the desert at Khartoum or Wadi Halfa. At the beginning of the return journey we were told that the de-icing fluid had frozen. Whether this was a joke I do not know. It did not feel like one.

When the family lived in Lagos and did not have a base in England, it was the Parker side of the family that bore the brunt of our comings and goings. It seems that there was a reservoir of family togetherness that Don was able to draw on. When we had a house of our own and were travelling to and from Uganda by air, it was Alice and Stan Prickett, who lived in Southall and were therefore convenient for Heathrow Airport, who would put us up as we passed through. Rex would walk over to Greenford, where his father lived above a shop in company with a vicious cat, and I would usually accompany him.

Martin returned to the Duke of York School, Nairobi and the girls settled down again at the Kampala School until it was time for Hilary to go to Eldoret Girls School. I got patterns and made all Hilary's school uniform, which included dresses, skirts and blouses for games etc. Margaret joined Hilary after two years.

I cannot remember the exact year we moved house, still on Namirembe, but with much more room, including four bedrooms, which meant we were able to accommodate guests who were passing through Kampala. There was a wide verandah all round the house and we used the side facing the view for breakfast and for my sewing room.

Whilst at the house, named "Golden Gates" by Patricia Thomas the previous occupant, we had two burglaries - one when the children were away at school and we had a guest, Vera Norton, in the guest room and a nursing sister from Mengo Hospital sleeping in another room in the daytime whilst she was on night duty because her own room was so noisy. I happened to wake up and go into the living room which I found stripped of curtains and cushion covers. The night nurse's room had been stripped of curtains, bedding and her clock, and Vera Morton had lost her suitcase and various other possessions. We found a trail of articles in the garden. When the police were called in they seemed to know who the thieves were and were able to return most of our possessions later.

Another night I heard a noise and on investigating found the door of the bedroom opening on to the front verandah open. The only article that we had left in that room for fear of burglary was the single bed and that had disappeared! We never saw that again.

I hated the children going away from home to school, but it did leave me freer to do some voluntary work which included going out to villages with a Mothers' Union worker (African) and teaching the women knitting and sewing. I also had a group of Ugandan women to whom I taught English. When Bishop (later Archbishop) Leslie Brown's secretary, Janet Evans, went on leave I was able to stand in for her. At this time I also acted as secretary to Leslie Minchin Clarke, who was the Mission Builder. When he went on leave I worked in the Mengo Hospital office part time for Dr Roy Billington.

Don was licensed by the Bishop of Uganda as Teacher of Women, in 1952, shortly after arriving. In addition to the activities she has listed, Don also did haircutting for many of the women missionaries. This also took place on the verandah. I do not know whether they paid her for this service.

We children had been brought up as part of a Christian family, expected to read our Bibles alongside Bible Reading Fellowship notes, to attend services and to prepare for confirmation. Our parents' religion did not fall into the category of Evangelical. At boarding school in Nairobi I was subjected to an offshoot of the Billy Graham campaign. It became obvious that my parents were not enthused about this approach and did not require me to have undergone a conversion experience for them to consider me a Christian. Nor were they High Church. Rex, who had again been licensed as a Lay Reader, would sometimes preach at evening services in the cathedral chapel. I remember listening to his preaching, but nothing else except the comparative brevity of his sermons, which would appear to indicate that they were not embarrassingly bad.

Rex had been recruited to become the new Manager of Uganda Bookshop in Kampala when Mr Dale retired, but Mr Dale did not really want to retire and he made things difficult for Rex and hung on and on. I do not really know the whole truth of the matter, but it seemed that Mr Dale resenting Rex as his successor complained to the Bishop and the Mission Secretary that Rex was not a suitable man for the job, although Rex had been Manager of a much bigger concern in Lagos. It was a very upsetting time as a man of Mr Dale's choice already in Uganda was appointed. Rex was transferred to the Diocesan Offices on Namirembe Hill where he was in charge of accounts and spent some of his time up country helping local church and school treasurers with their accounts. [This was in 1957] When it was time for home leave it was decided that Rex should apply to be taken on as a member of Attached Staff to the Church of Uganda which meant being interviewed at home. As it was not yet time for the girls' and Martin's end of term we decided that Rex should go home first and get all the transferring business done, and I should wait for the children.

Whilst waiting on Namirembe I got a bad attack of malaria and dysentery and was taken to the European Ward of Mengo Hospital. I was really very ill and when the girls returned from school they were horrified at my appearance. They had to stay with people on the Hill, and when I was well enough the Minchin Clarkes had me to stay to recuperate until it was time for use to fly home. Martin flew home later direct from school.

Rex bought an old Daimler car for £50, in good working order but with no means of heating. On the 1st November we set out in it for Newcastle to visit Nora and Tom and go across to Bill and Joyce at St Helens. We had a picnic lunch somewhere on the way and later Margaret discovered she had lost her wrist watch which must have been at the picnic site. We went on through worsening fog realising that we would have to spend the night somewhere. At Newark in very thick fog we bumped into the back of a van. The car radiator was ruined and after Rex had deposited us at the Railway Hotel he had the damage assessed. The car was a write-off, and the garage gave us £5 for it! We had to collect our luggage from it, including two stone hot water bottles used to heat the car a little. We spent a very restless night in a front bedroom of the hotel kept awake by cars and lorries changing gear for the hill on which the hotel was built. The next day we went on by train to Newcastle where we spent a pleasant few days with Nora, Tom, Pam and Lynne, and then went to St Helens to stay with Bill and Joyce. Bill was Vicar of St Helens, a very big church and parish. He had four curates, a Church Army sister and Church Army Captain working with him. One of his curates was a man from Nigeria who later became a Bishop in Nigeria. Bill and Joyce made us very welcome and we were able to go to a Sunday service at the very large parish church.

In 1961 Rex, Hilary, Margaret and I flew home to Temple Ewell. Martin had nine months to fill before going to Exeter College, Oxford, and he taught at Turi. He was to follow later. Rex and I were going back to Uganda for another tour, but Rex flew without me as we had arranged for Hilary and Margaret to go to board at Huyton College, Hilary having passed School Certificate, to go on to the next stage there, as she was hoping to get a maths degree. I went with Hilary and Margaret to stay with the Baileys at Ormskirk (where Bill was Vicar) to outfit them in Liverpool. We had chosen Huyton because the Baileys in the parish of Ormskirk had agreed to be their guardians when I returned to Kampala. As it was not necessary for me to return as soon as Hilary and Margaret went to Huyton, Miss Fenton, the Headmistress, asked me if I would stand in for a month in charge of the Sanatorium as the nurse had been delayed. This I agreed to do, so was able to see Hilary and Margaret settled in. During this time Clifford Martin, now Bishop of Liverpool, contacted me and arranged to collect and take me to supper with them at the Bishop's House, which was a very pleasant time recalling people and events at Christ Church, Croydon.

In 1963 I visited Don and Rex in Uganda for my 21st birthday. As soon as I came off the plane in Entebbe, the rich smell of the papyrus swamps around the airport came like a homely welcome.

Don and Rex left Uganda in 1964 and moved to Sheffield, where Rex became manager of SPCK's little bookshop and later worked in the Bursar's department at the university. He was again licensed as a Lay Reader.

Don never completed her autobiographical memoir. I suspect that this was because it was getting near to the point where she would have to write about the sudden death of Rex in 1977, and that was something that she could not bear to do. She lived for another 25 years after his death, keeping contact with old friends and making new ones, but without ever getting over her loss.

Unidentified bookshop scene, probably from Nigeria.

Part 7.

Reflections

In this section I offer my own comments, on the missionary life as experienced by my parents, on the relationships between missionaries, and on the dilemmas they faced.

Don's life in an isolated situation in south-eastern Nigeria would have been very different from life in urban Lagos, where a number of CMS staff and other missionaries were gathered. Both these settings were uncomfortably hot and disease-ridden for Europeans, but Lagos had more benefits. That in turn was different from Kampala, but in all three locations the culture was equally hard-working. There were changes over time as well as in place, particularly in communication. In the 1930s affordable communication was slow, and it was further restricted by the war. After the war the passage of people and messages gradually became faster. But there were continuing similarities. Looking back at life in Kampala, it seems to me that it was more of a colonial experience, albeit not a prosperous one, than a missionary experience, and there are elements in my parents' letters which suggest that much the same could be said of the years in Lagos. In Kampala we lived in a missionary enclave, which was a sort of outpost of the wider European community. I learned only a few words of Luganda and Swahili. Most of the Baganda that I met were servants, and although we were taught to treat them with respect, encountering a middle class black American was quite a culture shock. But my sister used to play tennis with a racially mixed group. At school in Kenya we were constantly exposed to our peers' implicit assumption that native Africans were inferior. In Kampala I probably had more contact with Gujarati shopkeepers than with Baganda, but those we did meet were usually friendly and helpful, even to the extent of giving lifts on lorries between towns.

Maybe the strong relationship between the missionary and the colonial experience should not be that surprising. Historically, the colonial and missionary efforts were usually linked. Don's memoir refers to Bishop Tucker, the first bishop to be at Namirembe. His autobiography shows that he considered the promotion of British interests to be second only to promoting the Kingdom of God. Later missionaries would not have been motivated in the same way, if only because they were working within the framework that the earlier efforts had established. But it was a common framework, and the colonial administrators had much in common with the missionaries, particularly in the field of education.

Rex seemed totally assimilated to the missionary community, and I was not at all conscious that he came from a background different from that of most of the people working alongside him. He had, in effect, completed the transition from working class to middle class that began when he went into clerical posts on leaving school and continued to gain qualifications. Although he was a lay reader he never aspired to ordination, unlike some other lay missionaries.

The missionary network was a scattered one, with concentrations in major centres, but relationships within it were strong. Don and Rex, in writing to each other, could assume that the other would be interested in having news of fellow-workers they hardly knew, and in receiving opinions of newcomers as they arrived. Each mission seems to have had its own way of doing things. Don's letters explain how things were done in the Niger mission, and why she thought some practices in the Lagos bookshop were better than those in the Port Harcourt one. In South Africa, where Don met people from other African missions, she might comment on their different ethos.

The great dilemma that my parents faced was to reconcile the demands of missionary activity and family life. The vocation that brought them together also tore them apart. After they were married and Rex's leave was over, they were separated for nearly two years, and some of Don's letters during this time are distressing to read. It is my impression that before her first child arrived, Don was disposed to give priority to her sense of mission, but after the birth her family had at least an equal, if not a greater, claim on her. I also have the impression that for Rex the family had second place, but his devotion to Don prevented him from continuing in Nigeria in the work he loved.

When our parents were at St Julian's considering whether to go to Uganda, the children were actually separate from them at Farleys, where I had my one experience of horse or pony riding. Nowadays most families would seek to involve the children in such a decision, but at that time it was not the normal way of doing things. I do not remember that we were consulted, but if we were I do not know what my reaction would have been. I was not particularly attracted to cold and overcrowded Britain, though from the time the family moved into the house in Temple Ewell (which was cold but roomy) I consistently regarded it as "home". The decision to go to Uganda kept the family mostly together, while allowing Rex, at least for a while, to continue in bookshop work.

To conclude this personal section are two poems, one written for my mother on her 90th birthday, the other on bringing the writing of this book to an end.

To Mother on her 90th birthday

You have remembered much of your story for us:
The locations strange to each other, the friends
Made and maintained, the brave decisions
Just mentioned as links. We have seen for ourselves
Your strength to continue.

In this calm shady suburb, what do they see,
Your neighbours? Perhaps some unusual belongings
But nothing besides that would let them suspect
Such a far-faring and faithful achievement,
Such strength to continue.

To My Father

Yes, trying to know and comprehend
Everything I didn't think to ask
And everything I didn't fully grasp
I ask around, and bring my questions to
The blank finality of death.

You
Are the admonition
At the back of my brain.
Such diligence as I find in me
Probably comes from you
(Along with the flare of rage) –
And, too, that aching sense
That my actions are not enough
And never can, ever, be
Enough.

So I poke and peer
Into those intimate thoughts
That survive in your writing
And your full life, partly recorded,
And I wonder, having sensed
This and that, how much more
Remains to be grasped and felt.

Bibliography

Hewitt, Gordon. The Problems of Success. A history of the Church Missionary Society 1910-1942 Vol I. London, SCM Press. 1971

Oldham, J H. Florence Allshorn and the story of St Julian's. London, SCM Press. 1951

Tucker, Alfred R. Eighteen Years in Uganda & East Africa Vol I. London, Edwin Arnold. 1908.

CMS archive. Box reference AF35/49 AFg E1.

Printed in the United Kingdom
by Lightning Source UK Ltd.
135236UK00001B/205/A